GET ONLINE

6 simple steps to launching
a **digital marketing strategy**
for the non-tech savvy

STACEY KEHOE

RETHINK PRESS

First published in Great Britain 2018
by Rethink Press (www.rethinkpress.com)

Contents

Introduction

MY STORY

I began my career in corporate travel, an industry that seemed glamorous and exciting. I wasn't academic and didn't perform well at school: a teacher suggested the travel industry. As a student who didn't get the grades to apply to university, I was intrigued. Observing successful business people travelling around the world, staying in exclusive hotels and attending corporate meetings was a life that felt unattainable and fascinating to me. I enjoyed the professionalism it required and the level of service that was expected. Specialising in corporate travel for the banking sector led to jobs based in the financial areas of Canary Wharf and Bank in the City of London. I thoroughly enjoyed my work for seven years – then in 2008 the credit crunch led to a series of redundancies.

It was during this time that I reassessed what I wanted to do in my life. I had frequently looked at marketing jobs in the travel sector, but they never paid enough to justify the move. However, during this time of financial turmoil, that was no longer an option anyway. There were very few work opportunities out there as many businesses were buckling down and trying to keep their heads above water, so I took a sales job: commission only sales, door-to-door in fact, selling telecommunication packages. As it turned out, I loved the work. I had the opportunity to meet people from all walks of life and it pushed me far outside my comfort zone, which gave me a huge sense of achievement. I liked the challenge of maintaining positivity at all times. Hundreds of doors slamming in my face each day built a tough skin. I've always worked hard, but nothing up until that point in my working life (or since) has pushed me to have such determined mental strength. It was a job that required almost no digital skills, which was refreshing. I spoke to customers all day, in their homes, where they filled out sales order forms, and I made a few phone calls to secure deals. I suppose it's a job that hasn't evolved in the last sixty years. The only difference is that being a door-to-door salesperson in the 1960s was considered respectable, but in today's modern world, the thought of having to have a face-to-face conversation with someone is much less attractive.

After little more than six months in this role, the sales agency I worked for offered me a recruitment position. They were impressed with my ability to explain the work in such a positive way and asked me to assist with scaling their sales force. It was 2010 and finding work in London at that time was still proving difficult for many. Few businesses were recruiting as the economy was still so unpredictable. I liked being able to offer work opportunities to people who had suffered redundancies, as I had. I was easy to relate to and it made the work very easy for me.

It was in this role that I became fascinated with branding and marketing. I realised that our ideal candidates were interested in understanding what working for us was like, so I began contributing content to a company blog. I showed what it was like behind the scenes and provided news items to a PR agency to raise the profile of the company. Before long, I had convinced my boss to let me take over the social media accounts and manage the company's website. The company's leadership team were sceptical and didn't consider any online activity important for their offline sales business. They were scared that I would spend huge amounts of money online and it would come back to harm the reputation of their business. However, they let me run with it for six months; I was outperforming on the recruitment side of the business and they were open to change and taking risks. The more awareness I drew to the business, the better candidates we recruited, the bigger clients we landed, and as I expected, revenue increased.

We were a door-to-door sales company dominating the digital space – something many of our competitors had failed to implement. Until now. One day, I received a call from a competitor based in Manchester: he asked what we were doing and how it was impacting the business. I explained the series of steps we went through, including improving our image and branding, revamping our website, investing in content and advertising and building a pipeline around our desired outcome. With my boss's approval, I began freelancing for this business – and others as they began to reach out.

Twelve months later I started my own digital marketing agency.

The corporate travel industry has never recovered from the financial crisis, not because business people no longer travel, but because there's no need for agents. The rise of the internet has replaced that role – we all book our own flights and accommodation now – much as e-commerce has replaced many door-to-door sales, customer service, and retail jobs. And there are many more industries experiencing the same conundrum.

I don't believe all face-to-face industries will die out, as we all need to do some element of our business offline. However, we've reached a point where everyone must embrace the digital world. Our clients, suppliers, and customers benefit from observing our digital brands. It helps to build credibility and provides an opportunity for research to be carried out at their own pace.

OUR MODERN WORLD: OFFLINE TO ONLINE

Marketing principles haven't changed much over the last few decades, but how we perform marketing has. Digital marketing levels the playing field: nowadays, a tiny start-up company located deep in the highlands of Scotland can reach the same audience as a multi-million-euro corporation in London. Small businesses can now market internationally and grow at a rapid pace by utilising modern technology.

As a business owner, you might have a successful business, enjoy talking to your customers in person, and receive a steady flow of referrals to your business: so why do you even need to consider digital marketing?

The world is changing at a rapid pace. From high-speed internet access to touchscreen smartphones which allow us to communicate with people around the world. These recent technological developments have changed the way we live our lives. In the modern world, you can't sit on a train or eat at a café without being surrounded by people with their eyes fixated on their smartphones. It's estimated that global internet users have exceeded 4.208 billion.[1] Globalisation and technology are accelerating both job creation and destruction. I have experienced both of these things myself. I lost multiple jobs due to evolving technology and have created and built a successful business through utilising the very thing that caused my redundancies back in 2008. The World Economic Forum estimates that 65% of children currently entering primary school will have jobs that don't yet exist. I find this statistic incredible – yet I fear traditional businesses that operate solely offline will get left behind. I worry that the little guys won't embrace these changes because they cling on to traditional processes.

When I launched my digital marketing agency, Brandlective Communications Ltd, in 2011, I did so with the ambition to help small- to medium-size enterprises (SMEs) transition their businesses online. SMEs have played a vital role in lifting the UK out of recession and are responsible for employing over 81% of the UK workforce.[2] It is crucial for small businesses to evolve and keep up with our modern world for the sake of our economy. I am passionate about helping companies embrace new technology and assisting with the development of their digital marketing strategies that take their business in a direction they never dreamed it could.

---

1 https://www.internetworldstats.com/stats.htm
2 https://www.makeitcheaper.com/blog/the-role-of-small-businesses-in-the-uk-economy

What can digital marketing do for your business?

The three most important things it offers business owners are:

1. A cost-effective route to your dream audience
2. Targeted advertising that you can measure
3. An opportunity to earn trust through your brand reputation

Perhaps you're happy with your traditional marketing and consider the evolving technology required overwhelming. I'm not suggesting you throw away your traditional marketing approach. No man is an island, and neither is a marketing campaign. Throughout this book, I will walk you through a simple methodology that you can use in conjunction with your existing efforts. Digital marketing can be used to enhance an already successful marketing process.

The ability to precisely target, interact with, and measure marketing in real time is a huge advantage and can be used to improve the ROI on your traditional marketing. Additionally, social media allows for real-time posts, interactions, and overall flexibility which isn't available with traditional marketing.

You'll notice I have a passion for traditional offline businesses. I'm not here to convince you that you should change your business model. I'll demonstrate examples of businesses that operate their core business offline and have successfully utilised a digital marketing strategy to scale their activities exponentially.

You'll meet Warren, a local painter and decorator who has doubled his revenue in twelve months; Seth, the owner of a rent-to-rent property business who spent less than £1,700 to secure a £39,000 contract; and Flori, the investor who raised a £12 million loan to fund a development project in Liverpool.

This book isn't for those satisfied with their existing marketing methods. If you don't want to change what you do, stop reading right now. If you're 100% content with the pace that your business is growing, then there's no need for you to continue. This book isn't magical: you won't triple your inbound leads just by reading it. But I will show you the six Cs of digital marketing that I use every day in my digital marketing business for clients across a range of industries. If you choose to implement these methods in your business, you will gain the attention of your perfect prospect through excellent positioning, attractive branding and intriguing content. You will obtain more visibility, acquire the contact details of prospects genuinely interested in your business and find techniques to nurture and educate them. Once you've built trust with these new prospects, you will have the ability to sell to them and enjoy a highly engaged audience online.

PART ONE

CHAPTER 1

What Is Digital Marketing?

Digital marketing is a broad term for all your online marketing efforts. Businesses just like yours leverage digital channels such as search engines, social media, email and their websites to connect with their existing and prospective customers.

The way people conduct research, educate themselves and buy products and services has changed. Unfortunately, this means that offline or traditional marketing isn't as effective as it used to be. The amount of time spent online has increased rapidly in recent years, with Generation Z the first generation to spend more time on smartphones than other devices. According to HubSpot, mobile now accounts for 52% of their daily online time – with an average of four hours and ten minutes spent connected to their phones every day.

While Generation Zs may not be your customers (yet), if you plan to be in business beyond the next five years, they will all soon become potential prospects that you need to keep up with, and digital marketing will play a significant role in this.

At a high level, digital marketing refers to advertising delivered through online channels. For example; search engines, websites, social media, email, and mobile apps. While the term digital marketing covers a wide range of marketing activities, some of the most prominent tactics and assets include the following.

TACTICS

Digital Marketing tactics are methods that can be used by any business to build their online profile, attract new prospects and nurture existing customers. When learning about each of these tactics and the benefits of each one, you will be able to build a marketing pipeline that is effective and generates the results you need.

Search Engine Optimisation (SEO)

The process of optimising your website to rank higher in search engine results pages, therefore increasing the amount of free (organic) traffic that your site receives.

Content marketing

The creation and promotion of content assets to generate exposure, awareness and lead generation for your business.

Social media marketing

The practice of sharing and promoting your brand and your content on social media channels to increase brand awareness, drive traffic and generate leads for your business.

Pay-Per-Click (PPC)

The method of driving traffic to a specific web page by paying a publisher to display an advert. Each time the advert is clicked, the publisher receives a payment. PPC adverts are commonly used by businesses on Facebook, Instagram, Twitter and Google.

Email marketing

Companies use email marketing as a way of nurturing their prospects and communicating with their audiences. It can be used to promote content, events, and products, or simply to keep customers informed of business developments and direct people towards the business's website.

Online PR

Online PR is the practice of securing earned online coverage with digital publications, blogs, and other content-based websites. This is similar to traditional PR, but in the online space.

Assets

Digital marketing assets are what you need to create in order to prove to your audience that you are knowledgeable in your area of expertise. They will work for you by offering advice and allowing new prospects to get to know you. These assets will position you in the mind of your ideal customers as the go-to person or business in your field.

- Branding assets (logos, fonts, etc)
- Website
- Blog posts
- Podcasts
- Downloads, eBooks, and white-papers
- Infographics
- Videos
- Interactive tools (quizzes, scorecards, tests)

- Social media channels (Facebook, YouTube, LinkedIn, Twitter, Instagram, etc)
- Earned online coverage (PR and reviews)

The six Cs methodology we cover in this book will show you which of these tactics and assets will be best for your unique business, and how to build them to appeal directly to your perfect customers.

CHAPTER 2

Your Personal Brand Vs A Business Brand

The question of using a personal brand vs a business brand can't be an either-or option. If you are the founder or Director of a business, your personal brand is intrinsically tied to the business brand and vice versa. Both are critical to each other's success.

Business owners frequently ask me whether they should build a digital marketing pipeline and branding for their business or themselves. They say: 'Should I be focusing the attention on myself like Elon Musk and Richard Branson? Or should I put the work into developing the credibility and authority for my business?' I respond with the most frustrating answer you will ever hear: 'It depends.' I know, it's annoying, but the truth is, it does depend. It depends on the industry you are in, the stage your business is at, whether you have a clear vision for your business and whether you stand for something passionately that is worth building a personal brand around. The good news is, there isn't a right or wrong answer: it's entirely dependent on what you want to do.

I have used my six Cs of digital marketing methodology to raise the profile of both personal brands and business brands. It's designed to create hype, build relationships and generate leads: the good news is whether you are a solopreneur, the founder of a start-up business or the CEO of an international corporation, this methodology can be leveraged. The same goes for business brands: whether your business is in a start-up phase, is a small-medium enterprise or a high-growth company these principles apply. As I've mentioned already, marketing principles haven't changed. What has changed is the way marketing is delivered, and the consumer's expectations. Whether you choose to start building this methodology around your personal brand or your business brand will be your choice.

My recommendation would be to pick just one brand to start with. Spend three to six months developing and building out the methodology we cover in this book before starting on the next brand. Marketing requires some heavy lifting in the early stages – there's a lot of deep thinking and discovery. While both brands will inevitably overlap and feed off each other, if you're starting out with your digital marketing journey choosing one to focus on, for now, will save you much confusion. When you have comfortably implemented this strategy for one, you can begin to incorporate the other brand.

CHAPTER 3

Why Digital Marketing

COMMON MISCONCEPTIONS

I have consistently seen three core issues facing those in SMEs when it comes to embracing digital marketing.

Digital marketing is expensive

Business owners often say digital marketing is too expensive. They think about the thousands of pounds they might need to spend and don't know how to justify the cost. I'll discuss how to assign a marketing budget in Chapter 6 of this book, but for now let's consider why digital marketing seems expensive. In my experience talking to hundreds of small business owners about digital marketing, the reason they draw this conclusion is because they don't build a pipeline around their core product. I network with investors and business owners all the time, and I've heard this statement many times.

At one such networking event I met Bob Jones. Bob is the owner of a property investment company in London. He was attempting to use digital marketing to source more investors to help fund his upcoming property projects. He had a case study which outlined his last property deal, and posted it on his social media accounts, and spent £500 on advertising to push the case study in front of a targeted audience that he thought might be interested in becoming investors in his next project. He received a small volume of clicks and downloads, but the phone never rang. Nobody called him to ask if they could invest in his next property deal. Bob assumes the £500 he spent on advertising and the time he spent writing and designing his case study was a complete waste. He said, 'I tried digital marketing and it didn't work, I spent money on advertising and it resulted in nothing.' I asked if I could look at the analytics for him and provide some feedback. At first, he claimed there was no point because it didn't work. However, I suggested that there is always something that can be learned from a failed campaign – it's always worth trying to understand what went wrong so that you can ensure the same mistakes aren't made in the future.

After reviewing the results, I told him, 'Bob, I've looked at your campaign and have a few ideas. First, I looked at your overall brand online. I Googled your name and your business name and could find very little information about you. When looking at your social media profiles, I see that your content is sporadic. You have posted some images and a few videos which is good, but there's not nearly enough consistency in your messaging. The case study that you are advertising is great, but it's the only thing I can see about you online. Once I download this case study, I have a phone number to call to discuss it. Your website looks nice but doesn't give me much detail about what you do. I feel like I need more. I need to know more about you and your business to feel like I can trust you. Your objective for the campaign is to find an investor who will lend you £95,000 for the next project you are working on. For a sophisticated investor, this may not be a huge amount of money. But for the demographic you are targeting with your adverts, it's a big commitment. These people don't know you. They have read this very impressive case study where you offered your last investor a 9% return on their loan. But how do they know that is even true? When they look at the other content you have posted over the last six months there is very little that backs up your case study. When approaching a new audience, it's very important to warm them up. They need to get to know you. They need to know what you stand for, what you believe, who you are and that you do what you say you do. If you are committed to generating leads online, you need to build a pipeline. You need to take your prospects on a journey with you.'

I asked Bob what would happen if he stood up at a networking event and said, 'Hello everyone, I am Bob Jones, I have an investment opportunity for you, I am looking for you to invest £95,000 in an upcoming property project I am working on', how many people do you think would say yes to this offer? People would approach Bob, and they would then want to have a conversation with him, verify his credentials, look at his previous investment deals, and speak to previous lenders to find out if Bob is trustworthy. They would likely go away and do a Google search to see what they could find and ensure there was nothing negative out there about him. In short, they would want to do their own due diligence and get to know him before making any decisions.

The digital space can help speed up this process for prospects because much of this information could be published online in the form of websites, downloadable documents, third-party platforms, social media, testimonials and recommendations on platforms such as LinkedIn.

Bob is not the only person to have had this experience. I speak to people every day who try to wing it online and are disappointed with the results. They put a budget into pay-per-click advertising or hire a social media marketer and hope for the best. The assumption that digital marketing is expensive comes from two things: not having a clear understanding of the value of the prospect you are trying to attract and only having tested parts of a marketing funnel. By understanding who your ideal prospects are and the true value they bring to your business, you can define how much can be spent on marketing to get results (more on this in the first C, Connect). It's also important to build out an entire marketing pipeline to ensure the best possible results are obtained.

Technology advances too quickly

Another common misconception I hear is that the world of digital marketing is vast and always evolving – it's impossible to keep up. After working with hundreds of businesses, I have found they are often unsure where to begin with their digital marketing strategies, or that something that was working very well twelve months ago no longer works for them. This can result in a lot of frustration around digital marketing. Here's my view: technology has helped digital marketing progress at a rapid pace. Change is something we must accept in almost all aspects of life, and it's our ability to evolve and adapt that makes human beings so remarkable. So rather than allowing technology to frustrate us, why not embrace it?

I was having a conversation with a client of mine recently about digital marketing. He is a successful business owner who I've worked with for over seven years. His business turnover is approaching £10 million and we were having dinner in a swanky London restaurant reminiscing on how different our businesses were when we first met. We were laughing about some of the techniques we used when we launched his first campaign and how odd they sound today. Warren owns a painting and decorating business and although he started out focusing on residential properties his core now comes from commercial contracts. Seven years ago, our approach to digital marketing for him was so simplistic. We were often posting photos on Facebook of the work he had completed with a link to the home page of his website. Back then, that did result in enquiries. It was in those early days of Facebook for business when organic reach was incredible. Fast-forward to now and it's nearly impossible to gain any traction without spending money on advertising. To think we would direct people to a generic page on the website compared to now when we have specific landing pages for all types of products. Each of those landing pages intrigues prospects to download or register for something and then we place them into a lead-nurturing pipeline that is full of educational, informative and helpful content before we even think about selling to them. The SEO work we were doing back then is another thing we joke about. It really was easier back then. Jamming as many keywords as we could into blog posts and metatags, we would measure to ensure each keyword or phrase made up at least 5% of the content. When we consider the complexity of today's techniques in comparison, we really should have invested more back then because it worked so well. Of course, today Google is so much smarter. Back then, we had a checklist of 48 must-do SEO tactics for each campaign, now we have 250+ and search engines such as Google are always updating algorithms. Warren agrees that this is a positive change. Although things aren't quite as simple as when we started working together, the new complexity allows a small business like his to outperform some of the bigger businesses in his sector. If the rules of the game are simple, everyone plays it the same way. If the rules are challenging to learn, you must be creative and strategic with your approach.

It's amusing to think how little we knew back then of what would exist in today's market. The complexity of today's digital landscape is incredible because our targeting is so much tighter and more niche – meaning we can get better results, faster. But it's that complexity that feels overwhelming to some people. I wish I could help business owners recognise that digital marketing is not something to be afraid of, and not something you should avoid because you don't fully understand it. The primary marketing principles haven't changed – how we can implement them has.

This has allowed an uprising of entrepreneurship and small business ownership. Think about this; multi-billion-dollar companies may only use TV advertising, but YouTube is for everyone; direct mail strategies can be translated into email marketing campaigns; networking is now done on social media platforms; podcasts have replaced radio advertising; and blogs provide us with information on any subject we could dream of, replacing traditional media such as newspapers and magazines. We don't have to be a huge corporation to afford to run successful marketing campaigns, these advancements in technology have levelled the playing field. Now, no matter the size of your business, you have an opportunity to get in front of hundreds of thousands of prospects – which is something that should be embraced.

Learning digital marketing takes too long

Many business owners believe they lack the time needed to create compelling marketing materials and structure a marketing pipeline that supports and nurtures new and existing prospects. As a regular speaker at business and investor events, I'm often approached by delegates who want to know how to create a digital marketing strategy for their business. I have landed many clients through these speaking engagements, but there are a vast amount of start-up businesses who aren't in a position to hire a marketing agency to do the work for them and are worried about how long it takes to create and implement a strategy that actually works. It was the sheer volume of enquiries that lead to the launch of my podcast and online training community, *The Vault,* and is the motivation for me writing this book.

Learning new techniques and digital tactics doesn't need to be scary. It can be as simple as learning in small chunks, then testing each new tactic out to see what works for your business. Keeping up to date with changes in technology can influence the time it takes to learn digital marketing, I won't deny that. However, there's a fundamental marketing principle that I use across all marketing campaigns for clients which I will cover throughout this book. By the end of reading this material, my aim is to help you feel confident enough to launch your own successful digital marketing campaign.

Influence

For anyone looking to grow their business and become known in their industry, influence will be important.

Influence is the power of having a significant effect on someone or something. Influencers are individuals who have the power to affect a purchase decision through their real or perceived authority, knowledge, association, position or relationship. Having influence is vital in any business because it builds credibility, authority and can lead to faster decision making.

Let's say you take your dog for a walk in the park. While watching your dog race up and down the hill, you're approached by another dog walker, a man in his late twenties. After chatting for a couple of minutes, he asks if you have 100k to invest in a new business opportunity. He's offering a high return. Would you invest with him? How do you think you would react? Your gut reaction would likely be to decline and walk away. Others may ask a series of questions. The objective of these questions is to understand how credible this individual might be: if they can be trusted and if they have a track record. After exchanging contact details with each other, you would likely walk home and do a quick Google search for this individual and conduct a bit of social media stalking to see what you can uncover about them.

Influence is not just an advantage, but a necessity for the savvy business owner. What happens when somebody Googles your name? What would I find if I Googled your business brand?

While some people are born with influence, the power of influence can, of course, be obtained. Credibility is acquired through recognition, the results you produce, and even the company you keep. Jim Rohn said, 'You are the average of the five people you spend the most time with.'

Influence is an essential part of the architecture of becoming a successful business owner. We can improve our influence by association alone. Have you ever found yourself impressed when seeing a photo of someone you know with a successful entrepreneur? I'm not talking about a celebrity; we all know those cheesy wannabe photos taken with a celebrity someone bumped into on the street. I'm talking about seeing an image of someone who you've recently met with a successful business person or highly influential investor. A photo that shows that they potentially hang out in the same circles and know each other. Isn't it interesting how that can change your perception of somebody?

Individuals with influence can inspire others to listen by conveying energy, enthusiasm, and optimism. To achieve success in business, it's important to hold credibility.

KNOW LIKE TRUST

The familiarity principle is something I use as part of my digital marketing strategy. It is also known as the mere exposure effect (which I will discuss later) by which people tend to develop a preference for things merely because they are familiar with them. In simple terms, the more we see and understand something, the more we like it, and therefore trust it.

Let's think about this in a context we all know. How do we as human beings make friends? A friendship starts by getting to *know* each other. A potential new friend must feel comfortable sharing (sometimes very personal) information with you.

Then, they begin to *like* you because of your personality, your sense of humour, and demeanour. Finally, they grow to *trust* that you have their best interests at heart and will be there for them in times of need.

The know, like, trust principle is a significant factor when it comes to building your digital marketing pipeline. To get your ideal customers to purchase from you, they must first know your brand, like your brand and trust your brand.

Know you

How do you become known?

This is actually easier to do online than it is with your traditional marketing campaigns. By utilising social media platforms, creating content that can be shared online, and demonstrating why you're the go-to brand for a niche sector, you will become familiar to your audience.

Here are some ideas for raising your visibility online:

- **Be clear on who you're targeting:** Don't try to be all things to all people. Pick your customer's biggest problem and focus in on that subject.

- **Be seen:** Ensure you have active social media accounts. Publish content regularly that provides the answer to your customer's problems.
- **Be generous:** Develop a free product that you give away that offers real value to your niche audience. Don't be afraid to give away your secret formula for achieving success – this helps them to understand your approach and positions you as an expert.
- **Be creative:** Consider how you can get in front of your customers. Produce video content, blogs, webinars and PDF downloads. By creating content in many different formats, your potential customers have a variety of ways to engage with you.
- **Be recognisable:** It's important that your prospects begin to recognise your brand. Ensure there is consistency in all of your visuals: the colours you use, the style of images, and the tone of voice.

Like you

Research conducted by the Advertising Research Foundation concluded that the emotion of likeability dictates whether an advertisement will increase a brand's sales.

Getting the prospect to like you comes down to being clear on what you stand for. It's about authenticity.

Will everyone like you? No, and that's ok. But you don't need everyone to become a customer. You need to appeal to the right prospects. The most challenging part of building the likeability factor is that customers need to like *you* more than what you sell.

Imagine two brands with an identical product available for purchase at an equal price.

One brand comes across as professional but somewhat impersonal. The other is bold, less polished, but shows you behind the scenes moments in the business. Which one are you more likely to do business with?

People do business with those that they know, like and trust. It is far easier to build a relationship with prospects by using your brand's personality than it is to compete on the price point. Use your personality to build a likeability factor.

Here are some ways to become more likeable online:

- **Be authentic:** If you come across as a dull, faceless brand, customers will find it difficult to relate to. Instead, boost your likeability by giving your brand some personality through storytelling; use a unique tone of voice and show prospects who you are and what you stand for.
- **Be engaging:** Invite prospects to have a two-way conversation and interact with you. Ask

questions, listen and respond with enthusiasm to what they have to say.

- **Be transparent:** Show examples of success stories and case studies. If you experience failures, talk about them and share what you have learned.
- **Be visual:** Share photos, graphics and videos. The more prospects that see what your brand looks, feels, and sounds like, the more familiar they will become with it.

The influential role of emotion in consumer purchase behaviour is well documented: MRI neuro-imagery shows that when evaluating brands, prospects primarily rely on emotions (personal feelings and experiences) rather than information (brand attributes, features and facts). Building this likeability factor is so important to ensuring your business is positively perceived.

Trust you

While delivering your precious content, you're not selling – but you are paving the road to eventually selling a product that's related to your content. For money to change hands, trust is imperative. Once you've established a reputation among your prospects as a knowledgeable, transparent brand, you can begin to publish content specifically designed to bolster your credibility. Customer testimonials, case studies, and behind the scenes material is critical here. Your aim is to show prospects you are completely transparent, that there are no skeletons in your closet, and why you are the best choice within your industry. When it comes to selling online, being known and liked alone are rarely enough – you need to become genuinely trusted.

The bigger your price tag, the deeper that trust needs to be. How do you get a buyer to trust you? In marketing terms, it's fairly straightforward. You're authentic, consistent, and follow through on what you say you will do. While all of that might sound simple, I've seen businesses fail miserably at it, time and time again.

Here are some examples of how to build trust online:

- **Be approachable:** Avoid using jargon or pompous language that your customer might not understand. If your prospects feel stupid, they won't want to enter a partnership with you. Build trust by showing them that working with you is easy.
- **Be honest:** Don't disappoint your prospects by breaking promises. Credibility is everything when building trust, so ensure that you deliver exceptional solutions to their problems. Always under-promote and over-deliver.
- **Be remarkable:** Give away some of your best advice. There is so much information online: if you want to stand out and be remembered, your free giveaways must be remarkable.

- **Be a no brainer:** Offer a free trial, a money-back guarantee, or a benefit that can't be found anywhere else. Taking the risk away from becoming a customer will result in a trusting relationship.

Know, like, and trust are the real things that affect how your ideal customers perceive your brand. Now you can begin to think about how to build a digital marketing pipeline that will lead more prospects to know, like and trust you.

CHAPTER 4

Reputation: Are You Trustworthy, Credible And Well-Known?

The term reputation refers to how your customers judge the financial, social, and environmental aspects of your business – and how this impacts their view of your brand.

The reputation of a business is essential to its survival. The level of trust a prospect has for a brand has a direct effect on a company's bottom line. There's an old proverb that says character is the story you tell about yourself; reputation is the story others write about you.

A well-known brand has the advantage here. Customers know they have a higher chance of satisfaction with a household brand because they care more about damaging their reputation. They are also less likely to regret their purchase decision.

Establishing your business as trustworthy and credible will attract customers to you and help them feel more comfortable doing business with you. Building a strong reputation is worthwhile as it can also lead to referrals in the future.

If your business has an excellent reputation in the marketplace, consumers will develop a preference for your company – even if similar businesses are offering the same products or services at different prices. The reputation of a business allows you to charge premium prices even when operating in highly competitive markets.

With the saturation of social media into every aspect of our world, companies are now more than ever being judged by their prospective and current customers. There is also the added risk of how former employees will represent your business online. I'm speaking to clients almost daily on how to actively build a good reputation, but also how to monitor future threats to that reputation and to create reputation management plans to avoid or mitigate them.

Before the age of social media platforms, the reputation of small businesses mostly relied on word of mouth or carefully cultivated campaigns by public relations and marketing firms. Those days are gone.

Maintaining the reputation of a company through social media can be managed internally; however, it does take time and effort. Employees and stakeholders must be educated and aware of a company's core values and key messages. Teaching everyone how to use a united and consistent brand voice through all communications should be prioritised when discussing reputation.

The reputation of your business will depend on a number of factors, including ensuring that you deliver on your promises to customers and vendors. Today's consumers value transparency and expect responsiveness.

To establish a strong reputation, start with the basics:

1. Educate your staff on what can and cannot be said on social media. Guidelines are helpful for teams as it won't leave any room for interpretation. Keeping them up to date with any new marketing campaigns helps to uphold their positive interpretation of the business.
2. Curate response templates for customer services issues online that no longer have the 'golden hour' to respond – now it's more like the golden minute. Without a well-crafted response ready to be published, you could miss an opportunity to immediately fix a customer problem – which could lead to significant damage to your brand.

Monitoring and responding to customers and resolving issues quickly will go a long way towards establishing a positive reputation for your business.

3. Take control of your online reputation. When a potential prospect conducts a search for your business online, your business website should be on the first page. Social media platform sites such as Twitter, Facebook, and LinkedIn should also appear. Creating a strong online presence is essential for successful businesses today. The more digital assets you own, the easier it will be for you to control your online reputation.
4. Monitor what people are saying about your business. Set up Google Alerts to track what is being said about your business online: it will alert you each time your brand name is mentioned on social media, blogs, websites, or any other online platform.

Maintaining a positive reputation is fundamental to the profitability, relevance, and existence of your business. Bad word of mouth, lack of response to a crisis and lack of transparency can rapidly decimate the reputation of a company.

CHAPTER 5

Digital Assets: Three Fundamentals

Before launching a marketing campaign, a business must have three core fundamentals in place. In fact, I won't even take on a client who doesn't have these three things, because the chance of their credibility being established is next to nothing. These are the absolute basics when it comes to building an online brand and essential in any marketing strategy.

1. Website
2. Intellectual property (IP)
3. Branding

These three things can be simple and don't need to be overwhelming, but they are essential.

WEBSITE

Some people in the digital space believe that websites are becoming less relevant with the rise of social media and apps. I have yet to see supporting evidence of this, and let's be honest: a basic website can be built in a few hours for minimal cost, so there's no reason for any business, big or small, to not have a website.

There are two reasons a website is a fundamental element when it comes to marketing. The first is that it shows your prospects that you are an established company, adding to your credibility and authority. Consider how you feel about a business that doesn't have a website. We often make the association that they're a small one-man-band type of business, and in the very early stages of starting the company. This can lead to questions about how stable your business is and whether you can be trusted.

The second reason a website is fundamental to your marketing campaign is that it's your home base. It's the one place all your prospects can go to get information about you. I know that if I visit a company's website, I'll be able to locate some necessary information about what they do, where they're located and how to contact them. It's a safe haven.

INTELLECTUAL PROPERTY (IP)

The definition of IP is an intangible property that is the result of creativity, such as patents or copyrights. This is important in business, and I recommend protecting yourself by registering logos, brand and product names, and patents. I own a handful of trademarks for different parts of my business, but this is not quite what I'm referring to when I suggest IP being a fundamental component of marketing. In fact, it's much more straightforward. When I refer to IP, I mean that I recommend you register the following components:

- Domain names (register business names, product names and your personal name)
- Social media handles

If you're investing time, money, and energy into building your online brand and a digital marketing strategy, how would you feel if suddenly someone hijacked your business? I can't stress enough how important it is to get these IP assets in place. Registering domain names and social media profiles (even if you're not planning on using them) is an easy and inexpensive way to protect your business's brand identity online.

BRANDING

Consistent branding helps maintain a strong visual component to your business: your brand should be recognisable and memorable. Keeping everything in a similar tone, style, and feel gives your business credibility, which will help your marketing be more effective. I recommend owning a set of brand guidelines: a set of tools and rules on how to use your branding elements. These instructions can be used by designers, writers, and anyone else using your brand's elements (like your logo) to create marketing materials.

Have you ever been viewing a social media page and thought, 'Wow, these images are amazing' or been reading a piece of content with real personality, and smiled? These are the sorts of things that should be included in your branding.

Your brand identity is defined by how your audience perceives you. A long-standing analogy is to view your brand as a person. Think about your ideal customer: instead of seeing them as a nameless, faceless crowd, focus on the one perfect individual client and think about how you could positively influence how they see you. You should share the same values, enrich each other's lives and be consistent in the way you communicate, the way you look and in the feeling that you give them.

CHAPTER 6

How Much Should You Spend On Digital Marketing?

When speaking to small business owners, I've found that most people expect digital marketing to be expensive. This can be true if you don't set clear objectives. The marketing industry would suggest that a small business whose turnover is under £5 million should spend 8% to 10% of their revenue on marketing. That number changes as company revenue increases. Businesses whose turnover exceeds £5 million typically spend 5% to 8% on marketing.

If we're adhering to this recommendation, for every £100,000 your business earns, between £8–10k should be reinvested in marketing to acquire more business.

How much you should spend on digital marketing is based almost entirely on the lifetime value of your customer. Once you know what a customer is worth to your business, and you have a clear plan for what you want to achieve, then you can decide how much you can spend on marketing to acquire that customer.

Whether you run a small business or a multi-million-pound corporation, marketing is essential to your profitability and growth. Knowing how much you have available to spend on marketing is critical; even more critical is how you spend it. Implementing a strategy will be important for budgeting. Your business's marketing budget should be a component of your marketing plan. You'll want to outline the costs of how you're going to achieve your marketing goals within a specific timeframe.

CUSTOMER LIFETIME VALUE

A common problem I see with small business owners is their inability to calculate the lifetime value of their customers. How can you know what to spend on marketing if you don't see the profit margin on each of your customers?

Understanding your customer's lifetime value must be a priority.

Before we dive into calculating the lifetime value of a customer, let's outline the key benefits of this figure to the future of your business, and specifically your digital marketing strategy. Knowing the lifetime value of a customer will enable your company to:

- Determine which customers to invest in
- Identify new customers and markets to target
- Agree on which product and service lines to promote
- Change pricing to extract more value
- Understand where to cut costs that are not generating growth

Many of my clients have been surprised by how many customers are unprofitable when they create a fully loaded estimate of customer profitability. However, businesses often shy away from this project – it can feel overwhelming. However, I want to reassure anyone looking to take on this task that while it may take time, it will be a valuable exercise.

First, calculate the overall customer spend over a specific duration of time. I advise using twelve months' worth of customer data to calculate their spend.

1. Work out how much your customers spend with you over twelve months.

Working out an individual's contribution to your business is easy. You can either take the price of the service you provide and multiply it by twelve, or consider the cost of the product you sell and multiply the average purchase amount over twelve months per customer.

2. Work out your company's expenditure per customer.

You must then determine the costs of servicing the customer, and the prices of the goods and services you provide them.

On top of this, you will also need to consider the marketing efforts put into customer acquisition, whether through advertising or discounts. This should be calculated on a yearly basis and then divided by the number of sales that took place.

These two costs to your business should then be subtracted from the overall revenue of each customer.

A word of warning: before subtracting from customer revenue, you should genuinely ask yourself the essential expenditures that have gone into a sale. While I have outlined the three key attributable costs (the costs of goods, the service and the average marketing spend), a range of other factors should be considered. Every business is different, and whether you are providing a service or product, it's essential to consider the time and money you are putting into each customer's purchase, sign up, or contract.

By understanding how much revenue will be earned from each customer you can decide how much can be spent on marketing.

How much would you be able to spend on a digital marketing strategy for a customer that generated you £12,500 per year?

COST OF ACQUISITION

The basic principles for working out the cost of acquiring a new customer can be calculated by dividing all the costs spent on acquisition (marketing expenses) by the number of customers acquired in the period the money was spent. I like to include the sales and marketing budgets together. The cost of obtaining a customer is the entire sales and marketing budget divided by the number of new customers acquired in a set period.

The cost of acquisition = sales and marketing costs / new customers won

If you spent £12,000 on marketing in a year (£1,000 per month) and acquired 100 customers in the same year, the cost of acquisition would be £120 per customer. Every business will be different. If you haven't spent any budget on acquiring customers to date, that's fine. Just understanding the lifetime value of the customer is sufficient for now. You can revisit the cost of acquisition after you've launched your first campaign and have done some testing.

All businesses are different, but you should strive to recover the cost of acquiring a customer within twelve months. If the average customer brings you £15,000 and stays for an average of five years (sixty months), the expectation would be to spend up to £3,000 to acquire new customers.

An ideal lifetime value of a customer (LTV) to cost to acquire a customer (CAC) ratio should not be lower than 3:1.

The value of a customer should be three times more than the cost of acquiring them. If the ratio is lower, you're spending too much. Businesses that have above average overheads should consider an LTV:CAC ratio closer to 5:1.

Disclaimer: Every business will have different circumstances to consider. My suggestions are based on industry averages.

You need to know these numbers. The more you understand what is currently driving your business, the better idea you'll have of how to grow your business through digital marketing.

CHAPTER 7

Introducing The Six Cs Of Digital Marketing

Many businesses overlook the importance of creating an entire marketing pipeline that allows their prospects to warm up to their brand. The six Cs methodology follows a structure to enable businesses growing their client base to plan, implement, and access a steady flow of new prospects within six to twelve months.

Through understanding how to connect with the ideal customer, creating the type of digital marketing material that will engage that customer, and captivating their attention on the right platforms, businesses following the six Cs model see a significant increase in the number of prospects captured. Once engaged, those prospects can be nurtured through conversation via email, social media, and a range of other marketing methods – allowing the trust factor to be built before converting to a paying customer.

Gain the attention of your perfect customers with a recognisable brand and a stack of engaging content and watch the powerful flow of inbound leads stream into your business. This methodology is designed to provide everyday companies with the expertise to rise above the noise, stand out from the crowd, and show their audience who they are.

A struggle for many business brands is getting in front of the right prospects. I have interviewed over 100 business owners and combined that research with the 500+ brands that I have worked with to reveal the common problems small businesses make in today's digital world. Nearly 34% of the business owners I spoke to believed that if they sent out enough sales letters, or promoted ads consistently on their Facebook page, then they would have prospects beating at their door, begging for their services. Unfortunately, in this noisy digital age, where consumers are bombarded with marketing messages, this is just not the case. These business owners find it difficult to keep up with evolving trends and technology, and quickly burn through their marketing budgets just trying to figure out the best way to engage their customers.

This led to the development of the six Cs of digital marketing methodology which is a tried-and-tested solution that breeds measurable results. By following this process businesses save time, money, and resources while building a steady flow of inbound leads to their business. These businesses typically grow at a predictable pace and become the go-to brand in their sector.

THE PRINCIPLES

Connect: Define your ideal prospect. Who do you want to attract? What do you want to accomplish?

Create: Determine your offer. How will you attract your audience? Do they respond best to written, visual, or audible content?

Captivate: Identify your channel. Which media channels will you use to promote this offer? How will you entice them?

Capture: Create your landing page. Will you offer a 'wow factor'? How will you get the prospect to take action?

Converse: Nurture the lead. How will you help prospects with their buying journey? Should email marketing or social media marketing be used?

Convert: Make the sale. How will you measure success? How will conversion be tracked and reported?

Each of these six Cs plays an important role and have been included in this methodology in a specific order. I have witnessed many small business owners do two or three of these Cs and wonder why their ROI is terrible. Usually, when I speak to these individuals about why they think digital marketing is so tough, it's because they're trying to take shortcuts.

CONNECT

It's important that consumers develop a connection to your brand by establishing a clear unique selling point (USP), a defined audience, and a recognisable brand.

Developing brand assets is essential. These can cover a range of things, but the basics should include having a strong mission statement and brand values. Your brand identity must look, sound and feel the same across your website, social media, and all marketing materials.

Whether you run a global corporation that specialises in buying and selling tropical islands, or a small business that sells organic and vegan macarons, without good branding anyone can quickly fall into obscurity. We are all busy people, and life doesn't allow us the patience to watch a twenty-minute video on why those macarons are so good before they make a purchase. We need snippets of information, delivered at first glance. A clever logo or exciting colour scheme can provide just as much information as a three-page mission statement if appropriately designed. Naturally, this falls short if we haven't communicated it through the right mediums or to the right audience. Working on the ideal customer profile and understanding where they spend time is essential. Throughout this step you will learn everything there is to know about your ideal customers, what motivates them, what challenges they are faced with and how you can best appeal to them.

CREATE

Once we know who our audience is, where they spend time and how they will interpret our brand, we need to create content to engage them. By making your brand accessible across multiple forms of media, you can pique your consumer's interest. It's important to produce content that can be repurposed and used across different mediums. Try to cover the four fundamental ways of consumption: written, visual, audible and actionable. Consider that everyone is different and likes to consume content in different ways. Not only that, but individuals may want to consume content in different ways depending on their schedules or the day of the week.

For example, I will happily sit and watch a video on a Sunday night from one of my favourite brands, however, on my Monday morning commute I would much rather listen to an audiobook or podcast. When my WIFI dips in and out on the London Underground, I am happy to read a 1,000-word blog post. On a Thursday, I dedicate a six-hour block of time to working on my business strategy, so taking action through the use of a strategy sheet I have downloaded or filling in a scorecard online to understand more about my business is perfect for those chunks of time. Each of us is different and has different preferences. When creating content, it's essential to plan different ways that your customer can interact with your brand.

CAPTIVATE

Now that we've created a batch of content, we must entice our audience to engage with it. This is the moment that all of our foundation work comes into play and we can finally get in front of our audience. In this step of planning a digital marketing strategy, your branding gets to shine, and we can use witty language to connect with our audience. Utilising social media to push our fantastic content in front of our ideal prospects is a huge part of the Captivate step. Organic reach no longer gives us the exposure it once did. We must identify which platforms will provide us with the best return on investment and begin a pay-per-click advertising campaign. It's scary the amount of information platforms such as Google and Facebook know about every one of us. But, as marketers, we must take advantage of this and use it to get in front of and captivate the very individuals that we identified in our ideal customer profile. This is where we use a lead magnet to prove our value to our audience and encourage them to pay attention to our brand.

CAPTURE

Deciding how to capture leads will have been identified in the first C, Connect. Whether you chose to use a landing page or pop-up form, it's now that this comes to life. By now, your audience should have seen your brand across all of the platforms they use and had an opportunity to interact with you in a variety of ways (written, visual, audible, actionable). Now that the trust has been built through giving away your best content, your ideal prospect should be ready to give you their contact information. At this point, I'm still a big advocate of offering something to customers in exchange for this information. This is where your lead magnet is essential. It must be highly valuable and bursting with information that your audience needs. Offer this to your prospects and capture their details.

CONVERSE

I often have conversations with business owners who do the first four Cs quite well. A common mistake is assuming that once you have their contact information they are a customer and will buy your product or service. This is just not the case. Now is the time to converse with your prospect: get to know them, offer them an insight into you and your business, and find out what they like. I love to do this through an email marketing campaign and across social media channels. The more content you can give away, the better you can create a wow factor before even trying to seduce them into a sale. You will see your conversions increase beyond what you ever could have imagined.

CONVERT

The final C is where we convert the prospect into a customer. It's possible to convert earlier in the pipeline depending on your business model, however, in my experience most prospects require time to build up their knowledge and trust with a business before they will make any significant commitment. If your product or service is a high-priced item, you should wait until this final C before attempting to sell anything. The goal is to build such a strong foundation with your prospects and take them on this fantastic journey of getting to know your business that it's only natural for them to become a customer. How you choose to convert a prospect to a customer is up to you. It might be possible for the transaction to be done digitally online, or for other businesses a sales call or in-person meeting may be required. By this point, you will know what feels right for your business.

When you're ready, let's take a look at the six Cs of digital marketing method.

PART TWO

CHAPTER 8

Connect

The first C is Connect. This includes defining your value, understanding your customers and communicating your USP effectively. It's about establishing a connection between your business vision and your ideal customers. Once you can clearly articulate what sets you apart from your competition, and how that fits in with the needs of your prospects, you will establish an unbreakable connection with your customers.

VALUE PROPOSITION

A value proposition is what differentiates a brand from its competitors. It could be that you offer the lowest cost, the highest quality, or the first-ever solution of its kind. Your value proposition could be thought of as what you have that competitors don't.

Before you can begin to develop your digital marketing pipeline, you must be clear on why prospects should choose you. This is especially important if your product or service is offered by many different businesses. Very few businesses are one of a kind.

Think about it: How many property investors favour a Houses of Multiple Occupation strategy? How many flooring suppliers are out there? How many plumbers are truly unique?

The key to creating an effective digital marketing strategy in this situation is what we call a value proposition. Unless you can pinpoint what makes your business unique in a competitive space, you cannot attract potential prospects effectively.

Developing your value proposition requires answering some probing questions:

- What makes me unique?
- What experience do I have that my competitors don't?
- What are five characteristics that describe my ideal customer?

- What are the top three benefits I offer my customers?
- What makes me better than my competitors?
- Could I narrow my niche and focus on a smaller group of prospects?
- How do customers find me online?

Many businesses make the mistake of trying to do everything. They want to do everything well, and they want to be all things to all people. They want to be known for having the highest quality products *and* the lowest prices. This is actually confusing for most people.

I build digital marketing strategies for entrepreneurs in the property sector. Think about this from the customer's standpoint. If you owned a property business and needed help with online marketing, wouldn't you be inclined to choose a business that specialises in the property sector, rather than a marketing person who works mostly in the music industry?

If you find defining your value proposition difficult, I recommend conducting a careful analysis of your competitors' ads and marketing messages.

For example, some airlines sell friendly service, while others sell on-time service. Waitrose sells luxury food brands, while Asda sells bargains.

Each of these is an example of a company that has found a value proposition to build its marketing strategy around. Consider how to manipulate one of the four Ps of marketing – price, product, promotion and place – to give your brand a market position that sets it apart from the competition.

I was recently speaking to the owner of a plumbing company. They are very successful and work on big commercial developments in London. I asked this business owner: how do you win these contracts? There are thousands of plumbers in London, how do you stand out from the crowd?

She explained,

> 'Well, firstly, I'm a female business owner, which is unique in this sector. I use this to my advantage by promoting my passion for increasing the number of women in trades. I have spoken at schools and at events about why I think this is important, which has given me a profile within the sector and has helped to build the company's credibility. Second, I leverage some of the jobs we have worked on. We highlight on our website and across our social media channels and in our brochure the high-profile projects we've worked on. I see many other plumbing businesses going to tender on these projects with a standard pitch and little-to-no USP. Our industry is one

> where pricing is fairly standard, so it's not something we can compete on – nor would I want to. We focus on positioning in the market, promoting our expertise and highlighting our big vision for the industry – which is to not only get more woman into the industry, but to also position plumbing as a respectable career choice. It's not a job for those that didn't finish high school; it is a sector that offers a highly profitable business opportunity. This is highly attractive to London developers.'

I absolutely loved her enthusiasm, and when listening to her passion for the trade, it's clear how she uses this as part of her business's value proposition. However, what could a small residential plumber do to separate himself from the crowd and develop a unique selling point?

Assuming price is not something that can offer much of a differentiator, my first idea would be around the personal story of the business owner. Is it a family business? How long have you been in business? Do you love working on problematic Victorian homes? Does your level of communication exceed industry standards? Do you donate a portion of your profits to a water-related charity?

A strong value proposition will help when designing your marketing campaign because you can thread this value through the content you are creating and continuously remind prospects why you are the best business for them to spend their hard-earned money with.

YOUR BIG REASON WHY

> Everyone has a Why. Your Why is the purpose, cause or belief that inspires you.
> – *Simon Sinek*

Why do you do what you do?

This is a very challenging question for many people. It's something that often changes over time, which is perhaps why it can be difficult to answer. Your why is the most important thing you can figure out when it comes to positioning your business. Getting clear on why you do what you do plays a significant role in helping to establish a connection with your prospects.

It was in my first sales job that I first encountered this question. My mentors told me that if I didn't have a big reason why, I would probably fail when the job got tough. I was in my early twenties and didn't really buy into this. At the time I was more motivated by proving them wrong.

Now that I run a number of different businesses, I genuinely understand the importance of this. Running a business is hard, and there are many ups and downs.

Moreover, many of us have experienced times when we ask ourselves, is this worth it? What am I doing? It's at these times that having a big reason why is essential. It's how we persevere through challenges. If you don't know the answer to this question, how will you ever fulfil your personal and professional dreams?

Defining your big reason why is essential for the following reasons:

- It provides you with guiding principles for what you do and how you do it
- It informs your prospects and customers of your reason for existing
- It determines your behaviour — what you do and how you do it
- It's reflected in your personal and company values
- It identifies the sort of customers that will connect with your business

When I start talking about this subject, many people ask me what my why is – and for me it's very simple. My passion is to level the playing field for businesses of all sizes. I firmly believe that anyone bold enough to put their ideas out into the world deserves a fair share of the limelight. It's my motivation for establishing my digital marketing agency. I love to help businesses who have big ideas and think outside the box. Those that have a passion for what they do. If I can contribute to their success by giving their brands visibility online, I feel a huge sense of accomplishment.

This clarity helps me every day and drives me to give as much as I can to support my clients.

Knowing your why gives you a filter to make choices, at work and at home, that will help you find greater fulfilment in all that you do. I am a huge fan of Simon Sinek, an unshakeable optimist who believes in a bright future and our ability to build it together. He discovered a remarkable pattern about how the greatest leaders and organisations think, act, and communicate. He claims,

> 'When an organisation starts with why, they stand for something bigger than any product, result, or metric. Their brand has real meaning and true value in the world. They are better able to attract and unite employees, customers, and partners. Also, their people love coming to work.'

When designing a digital marketing strategy, understanding a business's big reason why can help separate them from their competition and give their prospects a way of connecting with their brand. People buy from people – this is a common phrase used by sales representatives. The more a business brand can replicate the emotional benefits humans offer, the better their chance of success. In other words, if a business clearly articulates what they stand for and why they do what they do, the stronger their connection will be with their potential customers.

There is an art to be learned when establishing a connection with customers.

Here's a worrisome statistic. According to a Bain & Company study, 60-80% of customers who describe themselves as satisfied don't go back to do more business with the company that initially satisfied them. How and why does this happen? Often, it's due to a lack of connection. Customer satisfaction and loyalty mean nothing if your customers can't remember exactly who it was they did business with. Who was that company who double glazed your windows two years ago? Where was that little restaurant you ate at when visiting York last summer?

My memory is getting worse and worse as I get older, so to recall the businesses which I have had a great experience with requires a deep connection. They must make a memorable impact on me. And perhaps more importantly, I need to be able to find that business via a quick Google search with what small bits of information I can remember.

CONNECTING TO YOUR AUDIENCE

Big promise

Your value proposition, your big reason why, and your big promise. Aren't these all very similar?

They can be. However, it's important to invest time into how you would explain these. Write them down. Don't just think about them as you read through this book. Writing them down makes them tangible and can help you find clarity in these areas.

Your big promise is what you're going to give prospects if they choose to become a customer of yours. It's sometimes referred to as a purpose statement. The point of establishing this comes back to how you generate a connection with your customers. It's essential to get this right to give your prospects the confidence to buy from you, invest in you, or sign up and take action today.

Consider how you might take your customers on a journey to understand this big promise.

Ask yourself:

- Where does it come from?
- Is it bold enough to be remembered?
- What does it do for them?

- What does it do for the greater good?
- Can it be measured?

A good promise reflects careful consideration, courage, and creativity. The bolder and more precise the better. The best brand promises go big, challenge the status quo, and connect with consumers on a deep emotional level.

Many businesses I speak to often feel this part of the process is a bit cheesy, and some find it off-putting. Let me explain why I think it's so important.

Emotion is a fundamental component of almost all decisions we make. When we're confronted with a choice, emotions from previous and related experiences affix values to the options we are considering. These emotions create preferences which lead to our decisions. If, as business owners, we can attach a positive connotation to our business through a big promise, we have a higher chance of successfully converting a prospect into a long-term customer.

In the book *Corporate Culture and Performance,* John Kotter and James Heskett show that over a decade-long period, purposeful, value-driven companies outperform their counterparts in stock price by a factor of twelve. In the absence of purpose, a company's leadership is likely to have greater difficulty motivating employees and putting the company on a course to success. Customers are likely to have trouble connecting with the company. With purpose, a company can create positive value that is far greater than the sum of its parts.

Here are some of my favourite examples of big promises:

1. Dr Martin Luther King Jr.'s *I Have a Dream* speech. The big promise was America's promise of freedom and opportunity for all – no matter the colour of your skin. The passion he displayed clearly demonstrated his belief in this promise and set him apart as the leader of this movement.
2. Virgin Atlantic: to be genuine, fun, contemporary and different in everything we do at a reasonable price.
3. The Coca-Cola Company: to inspire moments of optimism, to create value and make a difference. The Share a Coke campaign clearly delivered the moments of optimism. Customers were delighted to find their own names printed on the labels during this 2013 campaign.
4. Chipotle: food with integrity. Chipotle promises to put thought into every ingredient that goes into their meals. Chipotle states their food is as real as it gets, and the great taste speaks for itself.

The word promise is a highly undermined word in today's society. This is where the old cliché actions speak louder than words is particularly true. A big promise is nothing if it's not followed through with action. The one thing successful businesses do well is deliver on their big promises consistently. No matter how significant or great your promise is, it will be lost on your audience if they don't connect with you. Solidifying a big promise for your business also helps gain credibility and authority. It can give the impression that you're a larger organisation than you are. This is not to say you want to mislead or misrepresent your prospects in any way, but rather to show that you have a more significant purpose and are goal driven. It shows that you have a bigger reason for existing than just obtaining them as a customer.

When you have a clear promise, you don't just attract more customers and opportunity; you also have a stronger connection with your customers, which results in greater rewards long-term.

RECOGNITION: CREATING A MEMORABLE BRAND

Branding is one of my favourite aspects of building a strong business profile. This is where a business comes to life – it becomes something visual and tangible. It includes what you see, what you hear and what you feel.

When it comes to creating a brand, establishing rules should be a top priority. This ensures you're building a unified, consistent and identifiable presence that translates both online and offline.

If you want your company to rise above the digital noise, a cold, sterile approach isn't going to cut it.

To get prospects excited about doing business with you, it's essential to develop a strong, memorable and warm-blooded brand. Regardless of whether you're a one-man-band, budding entrepreneur, start-up, small business or colossal corporation, I highly recommend building out a set of brand guidelines – even the smallest of companies can lose control of their identity without a proper set of guidelines.

Creating a visual brand will help your business be more memorable. For anyone that follows me or my podcast on social media, you'll know I'm an advocate of bold branding. Straying from the mould to elevate your company from your competition comes with risks, of course. However, in the words of hockey legend Wayne Gretzky: 'You miss 100% of the shots you don't take.'

Creating brand guidelines is something that a graphic designer can help you with, and I do strongly recommend you consider doing this. You can spend hours, weeks, even months, deciding on the design and ethos behind creating your perfect company, but if there are no brand guidelines to guide your team (and even yourself at times) your brand's values may be diluted. Consistency, however, is *the* most prominent issue.

Brand guidelines should consist of a comprehensive guide that outlines all the essential design tools required to create and distribute company communications. It shouldn't matter if you have a graphic designer or office administrator – you want a consistent understanding of what your agreed upon brand should look like.

From allowable typefaces to tone of voice, your brand guidelines should include the following:

- Value proposition, vision, and key values
- Purpose and mission statement
- Copywriting style, or tone of voice (personality)
- Logo usage
- Colour palette
- Font and typography style
- Image styles that work with the brand
- Marketing materials

Branding guidelines can also extend to:

- Design layouts and grids
- Social media etiquette and style

- Advertising treatments – when and where your business should be seen
- Business card and letterhead design
- Merchandising applications and options

Although they're a set of rules and regulations, brand guidelines should also have a certain degree of flexibility. There should be enough wiggle room for designers to be creative, while also being robust enough to keep your brand easily recognisable.

Before you can delve into creating brand guidelines, you must first design the brand.

Visual identity

When it comes to branding, a company's visual identity is the most crucial part. Colour plays such an undeniable role in branding – it can influence the tone of your brand, generate certain emotions or sentiments, and can make or break a brand.

Your first port of call when discussing colour is to make a note of colour theory, and which colours result in different emotional responses. You might notice that technology or finance companies use blues and cooler tones in their branding, or that health food brands often use greens and earthy browns. This is in part thanks to colour theory and the effect that these colours have on us.

Are you using the right font?

Fonts help convey your tone. Words may be exempt from visual branding, but not typography.

Use of language

We all know the value and importance of language and how certain words carry specific meaning. If you were to describe a car as *powerful*, this would attract people who want a faster, tougher car, but it may detract people who want a safer, more child-friendly model to drive their family around in.

Taglines and slogans

Following the discussion of language is taglines and slogans. These are incredibly useful tools; this careful compilation of words helps to explain what your company does, what your brand values are, and gives you space to get a little creative.

A good brand will create a tagline or slogan that stays with you and keeps you thinking beyond your encounter with the brand.

Tone of voice

Gone are the days where your only way to communicate with brands and organisations was out in public. Nowadays, brands have Twitter accounts and

Facebook pages, and consumers can interact with these brands from the privacy of their own homes. This constant communication between consumers and companies means that the tone carried throughout these conversations is a crucial part of the branding.

Personality and emotion

Picture a Coke ad in your mind. Did you picture young people drinking Coke on a beach or at a party, surrounded by friends, dancing, having fun? This is Coke's brand. This is what people buy when they reach for the red bottle of dark liquid – not always the taste or the price, but (somewhat subconsciously) they set out to buy the experience that they expect to have.

So, where do these expectations of experience originate? Yep, you guessed it: branding.

A good brand establishes an emotional connection with its consumers that often surpasses the product. Giving your brand a distinct and authentic personality helps it sit apart from the rest. This is the reason we often gravitate towards name-brand products even though the generic products are often just as good and more cost effective. We do this because these name-brand products have established some form of a connection with us through careful branding.

Good branding is trustworthy. It should make people feel at ease and be confident that your brand is the right choice. Know your audience and understand what would make them feel most comfortable trusting you.

Bonus material: take our online questionnaire to help you define your visual brand identity at www.getonlinebook.com/brand-guidelines.

CREATING A CUSTOMER PROFILE

Understanding your customers and creating a customer profile should be done in parallel with designing your brand. There is no point creating a fun, vibrant logo and colour scheme, and establishing a quirky, light-hearted tone of voice if your ideal customers are middle-aged, serious accountants who are very detail oriented and will spend the whole time trying to cut through the language to get to the facts.

To find your customers online and get your marketing material in front of them, you must first know who they are.

Building a customer profile is the perfect way to turn faceless potential prospects into real people you can market to. A customer profile is merely a detailed description of your target customer. Once you have one, you can use it to do things like market to and own a niche where you become the go-to business in your sector, or hone your marketing message, so it appeals to a specific person rather than a generic and broad message to everyone.

At a property investing conference in Glasgow in late 2017, I was challenged on my suggestion that every business must have a customer profile to focus on when producing content for marketing and social media advertising. While networking in the bar afterwards, another woman approached me to speak about niching. She said, 'I don't need a profile because my business appeals to everyone'; this statement is almost never true – but I hear it all the time. She continued, 'I run training workshops and everyone is a potential prospect, if everybody knew how to invest in property effectively they would do it.' This is simply not true, and if you think it is, you will fail miserably at digital marketing.

To market a product or service correctly, the first thing you must do is get clear on who your ideal customer is, where they spend time online, and what their challenges are. The biggest mistake I see businesses make is they try to be all things to all people and claim that 'anyone' could be their potential prospects. This is impossible, and causes many businesses to fail because they don't attract anyone. Many business owners and entrepreneurs I speak to about this are fearful of alienating individuals or missing out on prospects if they focus on a micro-niche. They fear that creating a customer profile that is too specific will result in our advertising campaigns not reaching enough people.

Unfortunately, many of those same business owners don't attract the right type of customers and waste vast amounts of money on marketing.

A customer profile is essential for every marketing campaign to be able to pinpoint the most effective marketing techniques that will result in measurable sales.

Among the numerous benefits of developing a profile, one of the most important benefits can include insight into what media platforms they are more inclined to use. Such knowledge may seem interchangeable at first glance, yet understanding when your ideal consumer is online and what their interests are will have a direct effect on your digital marketing techniques. Developing this further, understanding what media platforms your brand should be both present and active on will only increase your exposure to ideal customers that are interested in your goods or services.

The creation of a customer profile will allow you to control your advertising and ensure your budget is well spent rather than wasted on irrelevant platforms – a common pitfall for many start-up businesses. Your new customer profile will help you to pinpoint where to advertise and maximise your brand exposure.

As well as the benefits listed above, your profile will help you to fine-tune your product or services. The ability to anticipate consumer trends, needs and concerns will ensure you can replicate this within your product development. Generating this connection between your fictional customer and a real consumer will help to create a better understanding and subsequent ability to build consumer relationships.

Let's look at this from the customer's perspective for a moment.

Consider how you make purchase decisions. If you were seeking a grand and traditional four-tier wedding cake for your wedding day, you're not likely to visit your local bakery to have the cake made. You would look for a specialist wedding cake maker. It doesn't matter how experienced your local baker is, for a monumental day in your life, you're willing to pay for the specialities of a trusted wedding cake maker who understands the importance of this day, and has experience in creating, transporting, and building these cakes. You know that they will have overcome challenges in the past and will be fully equipped to handle any situation that may arise to ensure you have the perfect four-tier cake for your wedding day. Many couples will have more confidence in a cake maker who specialises in this niche than one who bakes cakes for any occasion.

From the cake maker's perspective, they will know that their customer profile is not everyone. It's likely to be females, aged twenty-five to forty-five, who are engaged, who either live or are getting married within a twenty-km radius of x location. They will likely be following x on social media and subscribe to x magazine.

Another example: if you own a plumbing business which is growing quickly, and you need help reviewing your business plan and growth strategy, would you be happy to hire a business coach who helps you to 'unlock your potential and empower you to be your absolute best'?

Not likely, as this is a broad statement that many of us don't understand. However, if you came across a business coach whose offer was Planning a 12-Month Business Growth Strategy for Tradespeople: Builders, Plumbers and Electricians, would that entice you to want to find out more about their service?

This business coach already knows what their customer profile is. It would most likely be a male, aged thirty to forty-five, tradesman, with ten staff, whose business turnover is currently £500k-£1m.

It's not to say that this business coach or wedding cake maker would never work with a customer outside of these criteria. It just means they can concentrate their marketing and advertising on a specific individual who fits their offerings.

There are many business owners and entrepreneurs out there who have no idea where to start with digital marketing. This overwhelming realisation paralyses them so much that they have no idea who they are trying to talk to or what they are trying to say.

Once you understand who your ideal customer is and can build a customer profile, you will then be able to determine the best places to advertise and which targeting options you'll use to reach your customers by listing the information you know about your ideal customer. Understanding your prospects inside out will allow you to:

- Increase conversion rates: you'll be able to say the things that will encourage your target customer to take action
- Attract more of the right customers: the wrong people won't be attracted by your message
- Avoid spending money on marketing that just doesn't work

To begin planning your customer profile, you'll need to define the following:

HINT: Think of one of your existing customers (who you love) when answering these questions.

BASICS

My ideal customer is [AGE]

My ideal customer earns [HOW MUCH]

My ideal customer lives [LOCATION]

My ideal customer is a [JOB TITLE]

My ideal customer is [MARRIED/HAS KIDS]

My ideal customer [HOBBIES] in their spare time

These basic demographics are useful when building your customer profile, especially if you will be using paid-advertising platforms such as Facebook, Instagram or even Google. Demographic information like age, gender and location will give your persona a look and feel.

CHALLENGES

My ideal customer struggles with [PROBLEM]

My perfect customer can't seem to [PROBLEM]

My ideal customer's biggest fear is [PAIN POINT]

My perfect customer would fail if [PAIN POINT]

These questions may drive your positioning. It will also assist with your copywriting and the advertising copy you'll use to compel your ideal customer to action.

INTERESTS

My ideal customer would read [BOOK], but no one else would.

My ideal customer would subscribe to [PODCAST], but no one else would.

My ideal customer would attend [EVENT], but no one else would.

The idea is to find the niche books, magazines, blogs, podcasts and events that your ideal customer would be attracted to – but no one else would.

For example, if you're seeking prospects to come on your property investing course – you wouldn't want to assign Kirstie Allsopp or Phil Spencer as a guru in your profile. They are TV stars that property investors are familiar with, however so is the general public.

Instead, choose more niche property entrepreneurs like Simon Zutshi, Rob Moore or Paul Preston. This will allow you to home in on an audience you already know are interested in training courses about investing in property.

I firmly believe that a successful marketing strategy should focus all your attention (and budget) on attracting the right people. With a detailed customer profile in your business toolbox, you'll be in the minority, as most business owners won't make the effort. This is your opportunity to develop a serious competitive advantage.

Creating a customer profile will allow you to tightly tailor your message to your ideal customer. The advantages to completing a detailed profile include:

- Creatively use the language your customers use
- Closely address their buying objections
- Design the sort of offer you know your customer will respond to
- Filter out the kind of person you don't want to work with

In addition, instead of guessing the most effective marketing approach, or the format your competitors are using, you can choose the method you know your target customers are most likely to look at.

As a result, you'll increase your conversion rate, attract more of the right customers, and avoid burning money on advertising that simply doesn't work.

(You can download a customer avatar worksheet from www.getonlinebook.com / resources.)

IDENTIFYING CUSTOMER PAIN POINTS

A common issue with digital marketing is targeting the right audience with the right content. It's not always easy to find prospects that need what you're offering. You need to ask yourself: what are your ideal customer's pain points?

By spending time understanding what their core problem is, you can build your marketing campaign around solving that problem. A product or service is only valuable to the degree in which it solves a problem and makes the customer's life better. It's your responsibility, and your duty, to identify these pain points and deliver products and services that solve them.

The more you can understand your customer's problems, the more likely you are to create a digital marketing strategy that appeals to them.

Actions to take:

1. Talk to your current customers. Ask them what they struggle with inside their business. Have a genuine interest in finding out what problems plague their lives and how you can help them.
2. If you don't have customers yet, take your efforts to Google. Find Frequently Asked Questions related to your industry. This is a good starting point. FAQs arise because they address common concerns of a general audience. However, they will be surface level, so use them to dig deeper.
3. Review your services or products – which of your customer's problems can you solve?

Identifying your customer's challenges is not necessarily an easy exercise. Perhaps your ideal customers don't know they have a problem that needs solving. Nevertheless, it's a valuable exercise which will be vital to the success of a digital marketing strategy.

I want to introduce you to three customers that I've helped build successful digital marketing pipelines.

Customer one

Seth is a rent-to-rent property entrepreneur. Rent-to-rent is where an individual or company rents a property from a landlord, and the landlord receives a fixed guaranteed rent. There are several ways to legally sublet a property, usually involving commercial or corporate tenancies, management agreements, leases or guaranteed rent schemes. Seth's customers are landlords. The type of landlords who want to hire Seth suffer from one or more of the following problems:

1. They've had a series of problem tenants who have damaged their property
2. Rent arrears: they are forever chasing rent payments
3. They've suffered from long vacancy periods between tenancies which have led to an unprofitable property investment
4. They are too busy to manage their own buy-to-let property
5. They are retiring and don't want the responsibility of managing the property

Common objections to the sale include: I'd rather use a well-known high-street agency to manage my property.

Customer two

Warren is the owner of a commercial painting business that was established in 1985. It's a family business that provides standard paint application from experienced painters through to specialist textures from their team of artists. The growing company can paint supermarkets nationwide as well as small bespoke feature walls in residential properties. Warren's ideal prospects are those that value high-quality work and are looking for on-going maintenance support. The type of customers who would seek to hire Warren may have experienced problems such as:

1. They've run into cowboy tradesman in previous jobs
2. They have a limited timeframe to get the paint job done
3. They have other tradesmen on the job, and communication between all parties is a challenge
4. They've dealt with unreliable tradesmen, and they don't know when they're working or who to contact if they don't show up on time
5. They have a lack of knowledge – for example, little understanding of the product specs and other materials on site

Common objections to the sale include: Other businesses charge 30% less.

Customer three

Flori is an investor and introducer who secures financing for property developers in West London. Her clients are usually focused on their developments, so her specialty is to show investors how each project is structured and devise multiple exit strategies for investors. As a third party, she sees each deal objectively and helps to find solutions for both her clients and investors.

Investors that work with Flori typically have the following problems:

1. They are overwhelmed and constantly pitched investment opportunities
2. They lack the time needed to review and investigate new investment opportunities and end up sticking with previous investment strategies
3. They have their criteria and/or formula for investments

Common objections to the sale include: They already have a small inner circle of contacts they trust.

Getting into the mindset of an individual customer isn't always easy, but it's incredibly useful. I usually find this step quite difficult to get small businesses to implement. While some business owners do have a clear understanding of their customer's problems, I will always suggest conducting more research and not just guessing what the main pain points are for your customers. Get on the phone with existing customers and speak to them. The profile that you create should be as detailed as possible, and outline the problems, worries, and considerations your customers have.

I speak to many businesses that skip this step, and instead address the problems they think their customers care about, rather than the reality. Making poor assumptions often plays a huge role in underperforming digital marketing campaigns. When using this approach, you only have half of the story. You can try to rephrase your marketing message to sound like you're addressing the customer, but if the customer doesn't care, this is pointless and wastes your time and money.

If you can truly spend the time to understand what problems your prospects encounter, you can build a solution for them. How much more likely are they to purchase from you if your service gives them precisely what they need?

This is so simple – but often overlooked. The sooner you can connect to new customers through their pain points the quicker you will improve the ROI of your entire marketing pipeline.

WHERE TO FIND YOUR CUSTOMERS

In the first C of marketing, Connect, we have discussed your value proposition and promise. This has allowed you to clearly define your unique selling point and show prospects how you think and what you stand for in the world. You will be considering your branding, including your colours, tone of voice and personality which will be used to speak to your prospects. We've also started to build out a detailed customer profile and create a list of your customer's most significant problems. Although this foundation model requires some deep thinking and may require you to adapt your existing strategy, you should already be clearer on how to improve your digital marketing strategy. The final part of this section is to establish how to find your customers in the digital space.

One reason digital marketing can be challenging for businesses is because they are advertising or publishing content on platforms that their customers don't use.

The first step is understanding which online platforms your customers are currently using, and this is simple – just ask! Spend some time speaking to your existing customers and ask which social media sites they use. Which online forums do they visit? How did they first hear about you?

This isn't rocket science, but you'd be surprised how many business owners guess this information or make assumptions. Assuming you know something about your customers is one of the worst things you can do. As you will have realised when creating your customer profile, your customers have interests and hobbies that could open up obscure communities online that might be a goldmine for you. One assumption you can make is that most customers, especially satisfied ones, will happily let you know how they ended up on your website or at your front door. Don't skip this step! Reach out to five customers and ask what are the top five apps or websites they spend the most time on (they don't need to be work or business related).

ACTION LIST: CONNECT

1. Define your USP or value proposition
2. Write down your big reason why
3. Create basic brand guidelines
4. Call five potential prospects to determine what their three core problems are
5. Call five existing customers to ask which online platforms they use
6. Build your customer profile

CHAPTER 9

Create

In the first C of marketing we have laid the foundations, and by now you should have a clearer idea of how to differentiate yourself from competitors, what your customer's biggest pain points are, and how you would like to position your brand to attract the right type of customers. Now is the time to begin creating the content that will entice them.

THE EVOLUTION OF THE RULE OF SEVEN

Traditional marketing techniques that pre-date the world of a digital and social media-oriented environment taught us that to efficiently portray our product or service to a potential customer, they must interact with our business at least seven times. This technique, known simply as the rule of seven, was every marketer's bread and butter dating back to the 1930s when the idea was developed by the mighty movie industry to fill up their theatre seats. Marketers quickly found that the importance of continually relaying a message was the key to turning prospects into paying customers, the hypothesis of which still stands true, only I believe the method has changed.

As with any strategy, the rule of seven has changed and evolved with time to match the needs of our modern lives. We must be savvier than ever before, particularly in a society that can consume media in real time, and at the touch of their fingertips. Today's consumers are more connected than ever before – constantly checking emails, social media apps, and even interacting online via voice technology. It's more important than ever to flood potential customers from every angle, and in as many different forms.

Research carried out by Braze found that when customers received outreach in two or more channels, levels of engagement were 166% higher than a single-channel rate and 642% higher than no messages whatsoever.

The modern rule of seven covers a vast range of consumable media formats and has evolved further to mean that we need to give prospects an average of seven hours of consumable content. This content should be consumed not just through one medium like that of the 1930s where billboards or posters were sufficient. A common way to describe this modern marketing concept is the term cross-channel marketing: an approach that allows brands to seamlessly communicate with consumers across multiple touch-points.

There are four primary categories that I recommend to SMEs: visual, audio, written and activity. I believe that the rule of seven still applies, but that we need to think outside the box regarding how we get that content in front of our ideal customers and provide multiple forms of content.

The following four categories should be considered for your marketing:

1. Visual: video, images, infographics, cinemographs, GIFs
2. Audio: audio books, podcasts, playlists
3. Written: blogs, white-papers, press releases, reviews, email marketing
4. Activity: worksheets, quizzes, scorecards, competitions, games

The idea behind the rule of seven is that continuous exposure to a company's message will result in the transition from prospect into paying customer.

How many times have you binged on content from a brand you were interested in? Whether it's obsessively listening to their podcast episodes, scrolling through hundreds of Instagram posts, downloading every worksheet you can find on a business's website or watching back-to-back videos on YouTube, at some point we've all gorged on content from a brand we love. So, consider what would happen if you have attracted a prospect to your business and they have nothing to read, nothing to listen to or watch, and no action to take because you have no content (or very outdated content). It's amazing what content will do for your business. It works for you 24/7. Office hours are irrelevant; if you have a customer who comes across your brand at 11.00pm one evening, you should aim to have stacks of content for them to obsess over so that you can keep them interested.

Don't allow this concept to overwhelm you. I will be giving you some examples of where to begin with your content creation. The most important thing is to start. If you can commit to creating one small piece of content per week, you will chip away and slowly build up a database of material that can be consumed by your ideal prospects.

Understanding where your specific customers spend time, as well as knowing what sort of content they like to consume, is very important for a digital marketing campaign. It's in these locations that you will want to invest your time, money and resources.

However, I would like to highlight that it's also important to do some foundation work by getting your business registered on some basic online platforms and ensure that you have a simple website before creating lots of new content. You can think of this stage like an audit. By looking at what you already have set up, you will have a clear idea of what you have to work with, and what needs improving to get in line with your newly defined brand, values and content strategy.

Identify the ways people are currently able to find your business online. Perform a search for your business with a search engine like Google and write down all the results that appear on the first page.

The results will usually fall into two main categories:

1. Pages that you've created
    - Your website
    - Blog
    - Social networks
2. Pages that were created by someone else
    - Online listings like Google My Business, Check-a-trade, etc
    - Review sites
    - Traditional media like newspapers

One recent study by Pew Internet found that 75% of consumers used a mobile device to get real-time location-based information on a business. Assuming you already have a website (if not, this should be a top priority), the first thing you should do is observe how it performs on your mobile device. There is nothing more frustrating than landing on a website that isn't compatible and is difficult to navigate on mobile. The attention span of consumers is reducing, so you must make the process of finding information easy for them or risk losing them to a competitor who has invested in a better performing website.

Consider adding a blog to your website if you don't already have one; this is a great way to add relevant and up-to-date information and advice for your prospects.

Social media can be a big hairy beast, and many businesses don't know where to begin. I'm often asked which platforms a business should be on and how to keep up to date with them. Register an account on as many of them as possible. It doesn't mean that you will use them all, but by claiming your profiles on all social media sites, you'll have control. Do this for both your business brand name and your own personal name. By doing this you won't be in danger of having a snotty teenager claiming the profile and posting all sorts of random content – and the same goes for competitors. Unfortunately, after working with hundreds of businesses, I have seen examples of companies being sabotaged by the competition in their market who have managed to register domain names or social media profiles in my clients' names. I've met many business owners who say that they don't want to claim all these profiles because they struggle to keep up with even one social network. Again, that's fine – but claim them and get them registered in your name so they won't be available for competitors, and you'll have the option to use this profile to redirect to where you actually want to deliver your content.

For example, if you've registered a Twitter profile and decide it's not the best platform for attracting your prospects, then you can pin an update to the top of the profile that says: 'This profile is not currently active, please visit our website to see our latest offers at www.brandlective.com'. You own the brand name on Twitter, which means if somebody does search specifically for you, they will find this page and know exactly where they can go to get more information. It's important to claim all of these accounts so you can at least have the opportunity to decide if they are used or not.

Additionally, if you do want to push customers towards a specific location or a core piece of content, utilise the about sections in all of these profiles to say that.

The next thing you want to observe is whether you're listed on any directories in your sector or area. Are there any more you could add yourself to? Is the information correct? Is the language and description in line with your new brand guidelines?

I always try to keep a log of all of these websites so that any time some of my contact information changes or I add a new service, I can refer to this log and quickly visit all of the directories to update the information. It's also worth noting that some websites will update this information across all directories for a small annual fee.

Are you listed on any review sites? It's common for review websites to automatically generate profiles for businesses based on listings in online directories or active social media profiles. It's important to claim these profiles and gain control of them so that you can add or update the information.

Over time you can build up your presence on these review sites. Each time you gain a new customer, ask them to review their experience with your business. This is a great way to build credibility.

Another way of raising your profile and building credibility is through media coverage. If you have some of this already, whether it's through local newspapers or big-time media, keep a log of where this information can be accessed. You may choose to feature it on your website, and I would encourage you to do so. Any third-party recognition or endorsement is evidence your new prospects can use to help them make a purchase decision. If you haven't achieved this yet, don't worry: there is plenty of time for that. If you're eager to get started on this, start building out a list of media contacts by getting a copy of a publication you're interested in and conducting a search online for the journalists or authors of the articles. Keep a record of their full name, area of expertise, email, Twitter handle, and phone number. Any time you have something newsworthy happen in your business you can reach out to them. As you can probably imagine, journalists receive hundreds if not thousands of pitches every day – so if you do decide to move forward with this, you will want to offer an exciting story. Rather than plugging your own business, try to provide an interesting insight or viewpoint about something in your industry. If you do get featured in a publication, they will almost always mention your business for context – so it can be a great way to earn credibility without looking like you're advertising.

It's important to get some of these basics implemented so that you know exactly where your business currently stands in the digital landscape. Auditing your company provides a starting point for creating the content that will add the most authority and credibility to your online profile.

An important thing to note when building your digital marketing pipeline is that it will likely change. As new trends emerge, or you receive further insight into what works for your prospects, your strategy will need to evolve. This is fine and can even be exciting. Don't allow it to overwhelm you; it's still essential to map out your marketing pipeline so that you have some direction. Without a map how do you get where you want to go?

I've had clients that over think this part of the process. They see all the foundation work they've done and believe every single nitty-gritty detail needs to be added to the plan. Even if you like to have very detail-oriented strategies, remember to try to allow yourself some flexibility. It's better to get a basic outline in place and start producing content than spend weeks deliberating over mapping out a perfect plan. It's much better to get started and create something rather than getting bogged down in details with no actual action. I know this can be challenging for some people, but there will always be time later to perfect the material – try to just start producing content.

I like to begin with the website. This is a topic widely debated among digital marketers: some believe websites won't be relevant in the future because consumers prefer to access information from social media sites and other third-party applications. I disagree with this theory for a few reasons. First, as a business owner myself, I always look at my assets. While you can build a brand asset across social media, at the end of the day, I don't own that platform. Instagram or LinkedIn could delete my accounts at any time, and that's entirely outside of my control. I met a lady recently who was building all of her content through Facebook Live. She had a growing number of followers, but one day Facebook deleted all her Live sessions without any explanation. She wasn't violating the terms of service and the malfunction was put down to a glitch in the system. Unfortunately for her, she wasn't building content across a series of platforms, so her online credibility was utterly wiped out. Although this is very rare, I still encourage clients to build content across multiple platforms and focus on storing most of your content on a platform you own, like your website. It's good practice to spread the risk by building assets across a series of different locations.

The second reason I still see value in websites is that I find my consumers like to have a central hub of necessary information. Even if I discover a new brand via a social network, I usually still end up on their site when I want to make a purchase or get in contact. I may come across a brand on Twitter, but I follow thousands of accounts on Twitter, so the likelihood of me remembering their name is slim. If I really like them, I might visit their website to find out if they have a Facebook page which I can like as I follow much less content on Facebook and use this platform every day – so I'm more likely to come across them again in the future when I have more time to make a purchase. If a company doesn't have a website as their hub, I might not remember to follow them on other platforms. Their website made it quick and easy for me to locate the information about them that I was interested in.

CONTENT CREATION: #THECONTENTWATERFALL

Think of your content pipeline as an outline of your principal business and customer needs. A detailed plan for how you will use content to address your customers is great – but if you're in the beginning stages of your business or this is your first campaign, don't get too bogged down in the details.

In the example below, I focused on two forms of content. You will remember from the first C that I discussed four primary types of content: written, visual, audible and action. If you're an established business, you certainly want to create as many variables as possible to ensure your prospects can consume information about you any way they like. But for beginners, start with choosing to follow my content waterfall method. It involves choosing one core piece of content to create, then choosing two ways to repurpose that item, and then three ways to distribute it.

#THECONTENTWATERFALL

The original storm: content creation

- Video interview
- Online webinar
- PowerPoint presentation

The big surge: repurposing

- Case studies
- Podcast
- Blog posts
- How-to guides
- Checklists
- Slide deck
- Infographic
- Social media cards
- One-minute video snippets
- Quote graphics
- Email campaign
- Newsletter

The major flood: distribution

- YouTube channel
- LinkedIn post
- LinkedIn articles
- Pinterest boards or pins
- Instagram story
- IGTV

- Instagram timeline
- Facebook posts
- Facebook Groups
- Facebook Live
- Twitter

The content waterfall is a process I established a few years ago to help get the most out of the rich content created for my clients. Essentially, it means starting with a really excellent core piece of content. My favourite is a video interview, but you could use a webinar or keynote that you've presented too.

When I do video interviews with clients, we usually spend forty-five minutes recording the interview and our goal is to get 170–190 pieces of content out of it. This may sound like a lot, but if you follow my process, you will see how easy that becomes with a little planning and practice.

The most important part of creating this first piece is preparation. Start with writing a list of thought-provoking, diverse and open-ended questions.

Here are some I've used before:

- What inspired you to start your business and how has your vision changed since?

- What is the biggest misconception about your industry?
- How would you explain your business to a five-year-old?
- How can novices learn and keep up to date with new trends in your industry?
- If I was to hire your company today, what would your onboarding process be like for me?
- What are some of your prospects' biggest fears prior to buying from you?
- What was the best project you worked on last year and why?
- What are three tips your ideal audience could implement on their own before hiring your services?
- Who would benefit the most from your product or services and why?
- Do you have a big, hairy, audacious goal beyond what you are offering in your business today?
- What are three words you would use to explain the personality of your brand and how do you portray that in your business?

To stay relevant to most industries, I've kept the above questions quite broad. I would encourage you to get creative and specific for your business or industry. Additionally, if you're looking to show some personality, you can throw in some weird, wacky or fun questions too.

The goal of this process is to pull out some unique and engaging content that your audience will find interesting and helpful.

Step one: the original storm – creating core content

You can choose to use a keynote talk, PowerPoint presentation, webinar or video for your core piece of content. In this example I will discuss video as it is one form of content that works for every type of business. I begin by setting up a video camera and asking clients these questions. I try not to let my clients overthink this too much. If they get stuck on a question, I just move on. I think it's great to speak straight to the camera, but if it feels awkward or uncomfortable then I'll get them to speak directly to me. My primary objective is to get this content to look and sound natural, so when implementing this for yourself, just do whatever feels best for you. It's worth noting that vision is our most dominant sense: most information transmitted to the human brain is visual. Any marketer will tell you that photos and graphics improve engagement, so imagine what moving images in the form of video can do for your business. Numbers show that staying out of the video production game may not be an option for companies, as it provides the most engagement over any other form of content by far.

The good news is your videos don't have to be perfect. It's the content that matters, so there's no need for you to be a video editor or spend lots of money on a videographer. There's a time and place for professional video, but for the sake of removing all excuses, I suggest beginning with your smartphone. Hubspot suggest that for most videos, the more simple and raw it is the more authentic the content seems... and that's what really matters to your audience.[3] Don't be concerned about hiring a videographer if your budget doesn't allow for it. Jump right in and start recording some short snippets and share your insights and knowledge with the world.

I'll record roughly forty-five minutes of footage – then my client gets on with their business and my team can focus on following our content waterfall process and generating hundreds of pieces of content.

This is what we call repurposing.

Step two: the big flood – repurposing content

In a perfect situation, we can take that original video recording, strip out the audio, and release it as a

3 https://blog.hubspot.com/marketing/video-marketing

podcast. If a really great insight or story has come out of the interview, we will write a press release which will be pitched to various media outlets in the appropriate industry.

I will then break down the original video recording into short video snippets. I can usually get six to ten short videos of one to two minutes each which reveal exciting insights for my client's audience. I would then use each of the topics in the videos as blog topics. Each blog will be 500-800 words, each expanding on the information recorded in the video and backed up by industry statistics and real-life examples. All of our blog posts follow a five-step structure which enables us to create graphics representing the five core points made through the post. Those five graphics can then be made into a SlideShare.

Remember when I said the key to getting the most out of this process is in the preparation? Well, if you asked the right questions, you'll have extracted a process or step-by-step guide. I would use this content to create either an infographic or a lead magnet which could be downloaded from your website in exchange for your prospects' contact details.

Going back to your original recording, listen for catchy or inspiration sound bites – each of these can be used to create quote graphics which you can share across social media. Each topic that you used for a blog can also be redrafted into an email and distributed as an email marketing series to raise awareness of your brand.

Using images effectively is one of the best ways for a small business to optimise their content and attract the attention of prospects. The first thing to do is make sure all the content has at least one relevant image: it's estimated that articles with images receive 94% more views and are forty times more likely to be shared on social media.

This statistic alone is a great reason to use images. As mentioned in the first C of marketing, Connect, getting some brand guidelines in place is crucial. It's very important for your imagery to represent your business accurately and along brand guidelines. Wherever possible use your own material, but licensed stock images can also be used. It's essential to own the material you are sharing. Subscriptions to stock image websites are relatively cheap and are well worth the investment. A word of warning: do not use images from Google search or any other platform that you do not own. This is a quick-fire way to run into copyright problems.

While using images is excellent for engagement via social media, I also recommend that you optimise the images correctly. This means renaming the image to include your keywords and brand name, and adding SEO elements like the alt and title text where possible.

Step three: the major flood – mass distribution

It's at this stage of the content creation process that I distribute everything across every platform my client is represented on. Each video snippet can be published across LinkedIn, IGTV, Facebook, and Twitter. Instagram, Snapchat and Facebook stories can be created to drive traffic to the main videos on each platform. Each blog post will be published on my client's website and third-party websites such as Medium. The blogs can also be released as LinkedIn articles and shared within relevant industry groups.

The five graphics from each blog post and the quote graphics that were created for each blog get posted across all social media channels over a series of weeks or months. Those same images can be submitted to Google images to index in the search results. I would begin a Pinterest board for each subject and upload the images to it. Each of the blogs will be broken down into twenty tweets and published on Twitter.

This is a merely a quick overview. My intention is to show you how content creation can be managed. The key is extracting the right information and having a good process in place to ensure you get the most out of the content you've invested in. Too often I'll see businesses pour money into creating a video for their business, posting it on their websites, and crossing their fingers hoping it will result in enquires. That just doesn't happen. A good rule of thumb is to invest 70% of resources into amplifying and gaining exposure for the great content that you're creating. For example, if you're looking at your monthly marketing budget, 30% should be invested in the creation of high-quality content, and the remaining 70% should be spent promoting and advertising that content.

Starting with these basic pieces of content will help bring your business exposure. If you've included all the elements of the first C, Connect, the content will also appeal to the right type of prospect. Remember, it's not about appealing to all people: it's better to have a highly engaged micro-niche than bland content that doesn't reach anyone that matters to your business. Some businesses worry about polarising certain customers, but it's the polarisation or niching that makes you highly attractive to your ideal prospects.

HOW TO GET NOTICED ONLINE (AND ATTRACT MORE CUSTOMERS)

Getting the attention of your prospects means getting inside their heads. It's essential to consider what they need, what their big problems are, and what they need to resolve those issues. Once you understand their pain points, you'll be in a better position to connect with them. Now that you have a content pipeline and have thought about the first few pieces of content to concentrate on, let's delve further into how to get noticed by your ideal prospects. If I had to choose two kinds of content that get the best results, I would say lead magnets and video content.

As discussed earlier, lead magnets can come in many different forms. The critical thing is that they must offer value. Don't be guilty of creating click bait which leaves your potential customer disappointed and misled. Create something of value that offers them a solution to their problem. This is very important in building trust with new prospects.

Let's go back to the rent-to-rent company. Their ideal customer is usually a thirty-five to sixty-five-year-old landlord, who is fed up with managing their own rental property located within a fifteen-mile radius of SW4, London. When considering what sort of lead magnet we should create to attract this type of prospect, we came up with the following examples:

- How to Avoid the Tenants from Hell
- What to Do if Your Tenant Falls into Rent Arrears
- How to Choose the Perfect Lettings Agency to Manage Your Property

By creating downloadable cheat sheets on these subjects, we niched into a topic that only a landlord would be interested in. If you don't own a buy-to-let property, you wouldn't be interested in learning 'How to Avoid the Tenants from Hell'. Problem tenants are a pain point that many landlords suffer, so we created a content-rich document that teaches them five strategies they can implement to ensure they avoid these types of tenants. I must stress, this is not a teaser. It's not to trick landlords into giving you their contact info in exchange for an obvious or flaky answer; the lead magnet available to download does actually teach the prospects how to avoid these types of tenants. Using lead magnets is about attracting your ideal candidates and building trust. Create value, not bait.

This company also runs training courses to teach other people how to start a business in the rent-to-rent sector, so we created the following lead magnet:

How to Source Rent-to-Rent Deals

In this lead magnet, the business gives away the pitch that they use in their business every day that has led to them sourcing more than fifty properties on five-year contracts in just eighteen months. This has had phenomenal results. As you can imagine, if you're looking to start a rent-to-rent business, this resource is invaluable. You would be blown away by the content and rave about it to all of your family and friends. It instantly makes this company memorable, likeable, and trustworthy. It means that later on in the marketing pipeline, when we get to promote one of their courses, you're open to the idea of booking and paying for their training.

Lead magnets, when used in the right way, are powerful. They should repel individuals who don't fit inside your perfect customer profile and be irresistible to those that do.

A lead magnet that has been very successful for my digital marketing agency is:

7 Digital Marketing Mistakes You Are Probably Making (and how to avoid them) [link to lead magnet]

It's one of our more gimmicky lead magnets, but it outperforms all of our other content. A word of warning on this, just because one magnet generates more leads than another one, doesn't always mean it's the best. A more niche topic may generate less engagement; however, the leads may be better qualified for your offering.

With that being said, this particular lead magnet is a good entry point for many of our prospects who then travel through the rest of our pipeline. It helps build awareness of our agency and exposes prospects to our six Cs methodology.

The reason video generates lots of hype and recognition online is because it offers prospects an opportunity to immerse themselves completely in a brand. They're visually stimulated, they can listen to an explanation of what they see, and it's often a great way to understand what the business is all about.

At my agency, we have a video editor and manager who suggests a couple of top tips for getting the best exposure:

1. Keep it short and sweet. Get your point across in a memorable fashion and encourage your audience to take the desired action (like, share, CTA).
2. Don't tease. Prospects want to consume content quickly and get to the point. They'll leave as soon as they get what they want.
3. Avoid words that give viewers a cue to leave ('Well, I think that just about...').

It's no secret that what appeals to one individual may not appeal to another. This is important to understand, and why utilising the first C, Connect, is so essential. By identifying who our ideal prospects are, we can use these insights to attract them.

If you've read any content marketing blogs in the past ten years, you'll be familiar with the phrase content is king.

Targeting content specifically to consumers makes perfect sense for a lead generation strategy. However,

I've met many business owners who struggle with this and are often unsure how to do it effectively. Why is content so important?

- It's a crucial pillar of modern SEO
- It helps you get noticed on social media
- It offers value to prospects and customers

Creating rich and clever content that educates and inspires doesn't need to be difficult.

Great content is the fuel that drives your digital marketing activities. To avoid feeling overwhelmed (which is common in entrepreneurs who are not naturally creative), we repurpose content. It works well for my team, and our clients love it. Essentially it means using one brainstorming session to create multiple pieces of content.

A few years ago, I had a client arrive at my office for a scheduled meeting. James is a business coach; he works with CEOs and leaders to equip their teams with tools and methodologies that allow them to make decisions quickly without distracting the core leadership teams. Our objective for the meeting was to come up with six relevant topics for his coaching business that we would expand into blogs. At the time, I would typically ask permission to record the brainstorming session. This allows my team of content writers to listen back when writing content to ensure we're using the right terminology – and it can also lead to additional ideas for content that we didn't pick up on during the live session.

On this occasion, our lapel microphone failed to work, and to avoid a delay I asked if we could video record the meeting for the same purpose. James agreed, and I set up my smartphone on a tripod to record James. In these sessions, we start with an interview. We work through a series of questions to learn more about the client, how they explain what they do, what benefits they offer their clients, and common challenges their clients face. We then delve into any initial ideas the client has for content – clients may have run into a specific problem in their business which sparked an idea that they want to focus on. More often than not, clients don't have the time to think about content marketing and haven't given it much thought before meeting with our team.

James has a lot of value in his head, but he doesn't have the time to work on content himself. He even lacks time to sit down for ten minutes and jot down a few ideas, so he values these monthly sessions with us. In just forty-five minutes we can extract what we need to create content, and he can go back to focusing on what he loves, working with his clients.

This particular session with James led to us evolving our extraction process to record not only audio but also video. From this one session, we were able to write eight blogs for his website, and each of those blogs was broken down into twenty tweets and five posts for LinkedIn. The key points from each blog were then turned into slides to share on SlideShare. Two of the blog topics followed a step-by-step process James uses every day in his business which we turned into two infographics. There were nine juicy sound bites or quotes from James that we turned into graphics to share across his social media channels and to a series of quote websites. We created ten short one-minute video snippets and stripped the audio from the video, which we saved for later with the goal of creating a podcast for his business.

Creating content doesn't need to be difficult. From this one forty-five-minute session with James, we were able to develop 170 pieces of content. There's no reason you can't follow this same process for your business. I have a rule for all of our content writers: a 600-word piece of written content must be able to be broken down into twenty interesting tweets. If it can't be done, the material is not rich enough and they must review and add more data, statistics, and sound bites. Try applying the same rules to your content.

Look at your customer's problems and write a list of subjects that would help your prospects understand what you do, but also offer the first step towards resolving this problem for them.

1. Record a video of yourself answering common questions or addressing current trends
2. Write a blog or article based on the core message discussed in the video
3. Break blog down into five interesting points for social media content
4. Turn the blog into twenty tweets

If you need to get your ideas on paper first before recording video or audio, that's completely fine. You could write the blog and then record yourself reading the blog or highlighting the top five points.

If you're still struggling with content ideas, I recommend revisiting your customer profiles thoroughly, ensuring each has enough detail to understand their habits and problems completely.

To summarise, the importance of continuous modification of your marketing leads is essential to building a successful business. Offering content that is relevant to your audience helps them see you as a valuable source of information. On top of that, original content makes it less likely that they will tune you out. Creating content that solves your typical prospects' problems is necessary for turning potential customers into paying consumers and is something you should incorporate into your marketing pipeline.

ACTION LIST: CREATE

1. Audit your digital brand
2. Launch or review your website
3. Claim your social media profiles
4. Complete your marketing pipeline blueprint
5. Write a list of five topics your customers need help with
6. Book a photoshoot

CHAPTER 10

Captivate

GO TO MARKET

This part is the implementation of my six Cs methodology. At this point in your pipeline you will have identified and started to create the content your prospects will be interested in and will need to look at how to get it out into the world and in front of these potential prospects.

Utilising social media to publish fantastic content to reach your ideal prospects is a huge part of the Captivate step. This is the moment that all your foundation work comes into play and you can finally get in front of your audience. This is when your branding gets to shine, and you can use the content you've been creating to connect with your audience.

The familiarity principle

You've likely experienced hearing a new song on the radio and at first not enjoying it, but after hearing it many times, you catch yourself humming along to it when you least expect.

This phenomenon is one example of the familiarity principle, also known as the mere exposure effect. The more you see or hear something, the more you like it. In other words, we tend to like things more when they're familiar to us.

Studies have shown that we're all attracted to what is familiar to us, and that repeated exposure to individual people will increase our attraction towards them. This is a subconscious process.

We usually aren't even aware of making such a choice. We are attracted to familiar people because we consider them safe and unlikely to cause harm. This same principle applies to marketing and branding. The exposure effect is sometimes also linked to subliminal messaging: repeated exposure to a product, to associate a positive effect to it, is, in fact, the most common approach in advertising. Brands of cars, technology, drinks and other products appear clearly in video segments without giving the impression of watching a commercial.

Consider BMW's Mini Cooper in *The Italian Job* (2003). The real star of *The Italian Job* is not a person, but a car. The famous car chase scene featured three BMW Mini Coopers in three different colours. The original 1969 film featured an old model of Mini Cooper, so when the film's producers asked BMW if they could use the newer model for the remake, they agreed – and provided more than thirty cars for use in the movie. And it worked: BMW saw a 22% increase in sales in the year the film was released.

Another example of how the familiarity principle works in this context is when a popular TV series replaces an actor. Have you ever been watching a TV series and halfway through an actor is switched?

The Fresh Prince of Bel Air decided to replace Vivian Banks three years into the show. *That '70s Show* recast the role of Laurie Forman for the final year. Ross Gellar's ex-wife in *Friends,* Carol, was replaced during season one. If you're a fan of any of these shows, you may have felt shocked or disappointed that these actors were switched out and the producers hoped you wouldn't notice. It's not that the replacement wasn't a great actor necessarily, but it feels uncomfortable because you've become familiar with the character. But sure enough, as you're continually exposed to that new actor, you warm to them, and eventually forget that they were not the original.

This familiarity principle is exciting and plays a crucial role in marketing as it exploits the psychological underpinnings of human decision making. A simple way to take advantage of this exposure effect is to show your prospects your unique selling point (USP) over and over again.

The more you feature your USP, talk about your USP, rave about your USP and display your USP, the more familiar your audience will become with your business.

More exposure leads to familiarity, which leads to comfort, which results in remarkable rates of conversion as a whole.

Overall, these examples show how becoming familiar with something or someone can be enough to make us like that thing or brand more. I always tell people that it's worth showing up to social events – it can be a simple way to become a familiar (and likeable) face. Use the familiarity principle or exposure effect to improve your conversions by displaying your brand in many different ways to your ideal prospects. Use social media to your advantage, provide multiple types of content, including videos, images, blogs, books and podcasts.

A word of warning when using the exposure effect: don't push the same advertisement in front of your audience over and over again. It's essential for them to see it multiple times, but consider how you can position the content in different ways. Repeated content can have an adverse effect if the positioning isn't perfect. Similarly, if you're targeting the wrong audience, this can negatively impact the perception of your brand. Once again, this illustrates the foundations highlighted in step one, Connect.

Here's an example of how we used the familiarity principle in a recent marketing campaign for a property training event. It was a one-day event, and it was the first one of its kind in the rent-to-rent sector. We had an excellent USP and a central London location for the venue. The one concern from the company was that because it was the first event, there was no content to leverage. They were concerned that without historical case studies it wouldn't be a success. On the contrary, we were able to locate six well-known property investors who had done business with this company over the past two years, each of which were more than happy to provide video testimonials of their experience working with them. These endorsements added credibility to the facilitator of the event and provided the confidence needed for prospects to sign up. Additionally, there were multiple speakers throughout the day, each of which had their own audience and industry authority which we were able to demonstrate in the digital brochure we produced for the event, and across the advertisements we ran online. In this example, we used well-known, successful, and familiar people in the industry to build trust with the target audience. We were able to leverage the familiarity of these individuals to add credibility to the event. This, combined with a twelve-week pay-per-click campaign which gave the event visibility, led to the event being sold out three weeks before it took place.

Consider how you could use the exposure effect in your marketing and take advantage of its powerful ability to increase trust with your brand.

UTILISING SOCIAL MEDIA

If you're a business using social media, you've probably noticed that reaching new customers organically, without paying for advertising, is becoming increasingly difficult. Gone are the days when just posting content on your timeline would generate a steady flow of leads.

The decline of organic reach is mainly due to the volume of content being shared across social media, blogs and websites. As more content is created and shared online, individual pieces of content have less time to make an impact before they are swallowed up by newer, more relevant content.

Two dominating factors have paved the way for this decline. The first is that following or liking a business page on any of the major social media sites doesn't automatically mean that a user will then see every update from that company on their newsfeed.

Many social media sites have openly revealed how they filter newsfeeds in the past, stating that algorithms are in place to avoid overloading users with more content than they could digest in a day. On average, these algorithms filter your newsfeed to contain around 300 posts; these posts are selected according to how often a user interacts with particular people or pages, the popularity of the posts (how many likes or shares they've received), and whether a user has responded well to similar content in the past.

The second factor is simply that social media is becoming oversaturated with businesses vying for consumer attention. Although these algorithms have been put in place to improve user experience, for SMEs, it has made it incredibly difficult to get in front of new consumers just by posting content.

Now we must pay for that benefit.

When speaking to business owners at networking events, I've observed that many people believe pay-per-click advertising is expensive.

I was speaking one evening to Charles, a property developer in London. He said, 'I'm curious to know how you use social media and Google to advertise, because each time I've tried it, I've spent loads of money and it hasn't resulted in anything.' I asked him who his ideal prospect was, and he responded with a vague answer along the lines of 'anyone across the country who has a minimum of £150,000 to invest'. I asked him what he knew about this type of person. What were their problems when it came to investing, and how much was his business willing to spend to acquire such an investor? He was puzzled by these questions. Pay-per-click advertisers will take as much money as you will give them and push your adverts out in front of as many people as possible – which inevitably means you will burn through your budget (which he later told me was £100) in less than twenty-four hours if you're not careful.

I find these sorts of conversations amusing, because for some reason people expect a small advertising budget to result in leads flooding into their business. It's just not how it works.

This is why I stress how important it is to look at the entire pipeline and invest in planning. If Charles had known how much revenue the investor would generate him on this new development, he would have had a clear picture of how much could be spent on advertising to acquire that customer. If he had a deep understanding of what motivated or caused pain to his ideal investor, he could have created a lead magnet that addressed those things. If Charles had a more detailed customer profile, the targeting on the advert could be more niche. The more you understand your ideal prospects, the easier and cheaper pay-per-click advertising becomes.

I hope to be able to bust the myth that pay-per-click advertising is expensive by showing you this example.

The rent-to-rent company we spoke about earlier set a budget of £400 per month for advertising. We built a strong social media presence with lots of branded content that was recognisable and interesting. We worked with the company to produce a strong customer profile and created some lead magnets that solved their customer's core problems with renting out their property. Additionally, we know the following about the company:

- **Location:** they will only take on properties within a fifteen-mile radius of SW4
- **Behaviours:** add data/content from Facebook
- **Interests:** property insurance, buy-to-let, home renovation shows, real estate development, real estate trends, property management, landlords, home renovations, real estate investing, property damage, property managers

Putting the work into understanding who needs to be reached via the pay-per-click adverts and investing in creating the content necessary to attract this type of prospect, left us ready to launch these ads. We know from running this campaign for twelve months that the average cost per lead is £11.25. We also know that for every thirty-five leads, the rent-to-rent company gets three viewings at properties that meet their specific requirements and their current conversion rate is 1:3.

The cost of acquiring a rent-to-rent deal via pay-per-click advertising (excluding the expenses involved in the research and production of marketing materials such as the lead magnet and their sales agent's hourly pay) is £400. The average deal generates £34,000 over five years. If you could make £34,000 in profit for an investment of £400 in advertising, would you still think it was expensive?

You must plan. I've seen many business owners just like Charles looking for a quick win, throwing money willy-nilly into advertising to see what happens. This is a terrible idea and will rarely result in your desired outcome. Spend time understanding your prospects and developing content for them that offers real value.

PPC: FACEBOOK ADVERTISING VS GOOGLE ADWORDS

Just like traditional media channels such as TV commercials, radio spots, and print ads, your results are going to be minimal at best if you broadcast your message to the wrong audience. Thankfully, by the time you reach this step in your marketing pipeline, you will have a clear value proposition, and understand who your customer is and what their core problems are. You will have mapped out your marketing pipeline and begun creating a stock of content to push out to your audience. The best way to get directly in front of your audience is targeted advertising – and the best way to achieve this is with PPC advertising.

PPC stands for pay-per-click advertising. It's used to describe the adverts that are available to run across search engines such as Google and Bing, and also to describe social media advertising on platforms such as Facebook, Instagram, Twitter and LinkedIn.

I want to highlight that carrying out a PPC advertising campaign differs significantly between search engines and social media platforms.

Consider what you use these websites to achieve. You visit a search engine to search for the answer to a problem. You visit a social media platform to see what your friends are doing and to see beautiful images and engaging videos from brands that you admire (although many social media platforms are working towards becoming search engines, that hasn't quite happened yet).

It's important to understand how we use these websites because your approach to using their advertising services will be different.

I will focus my explanation of social media pay-per-click advertising around Facebook to keep it simple. The principles will be the same for other social media platforms, though the content may differ. For now, I'm only discussing the principles of advertising. With Facebook and other social media platforms or apps, we will be using demographics, behaviours and interests to target potential prospects. Your customer profile is essential for this type of advertising.

PPC carried out on social media is a long game when compared to PPC on search engines. This is because the customer hasn't specifically searched for what you offer. Instead, you're putting a solution in front of your ideal prospects based on their demographics, online behaviours, and their interests as recorded by the social media site based on previous activity. You may think you'll get a better ROI from a PPC advertisement via a search engine like Google, simply because you know that the prospect has specifically searched for a solution and is ready to buy. However, there is much to be said for branding, relationship marketing, and the familiarity principle when it comes to converting prospects into customers that social media advertising offers. In addition to the written content in a social media advertisement, you can also use videos and images to captivate your customers. Social media advertising should be thought of as a long game. It's an incredible tool for brand awareness and is very useful for engaging your ideal prospect, which you will then push through the rest of your marketing pipeline to allow them to get to know you, like you, and trust you. A lot of nurturing and conversations will need to be had with the leads generated through social media advertising before the lead converts into a paying customer.

For businesses operating in a highly saturated industry, social media advertising offers a further advantage. The cost-per-click on search engine advertising can be very high for a highly competitive subject. For example, the most expensive keywords in Google AdWords and Bing Ads cost fifty GBP or more per click. These are generally highly competitive keywords in industries that have high customer lifetime values, like law and insurance. If you operate in a highly competitive sector with a high customer lifetime value, but perhaps your budget doesn't stretch this far, social media advertising may be more useful for your business. You can build up relationships, give away great content, and build trust before attempting to sell your products and services.

I love using Facebook advertising for captivating an audience and building brand awareness. It also plays a vital role in developing our email list and capturing contact details in exchange for high-value downloads.

PPC advertising carried out via search engines is a different form of advertising and should be implemented with a different approach. In many cases, it can offer quick wins: prospects will come across these adverts when searching for a specific keyword or phrase in a search engine. For the sake of keeping my explanation simple, let's focus on Google.

Google allows for some demographic- and interest-based targeting, but not quite to the level of personal details that Facebook does. Google AdWords is based on an auction system. It's a common misconception that the most significant budget wins when it comes to Google AdWords: it's not that simple. Google AdWords rewards businesses who have high-quality ad campaigns with lower costs and better ad placement. The ad auction begins when a user enters a phrase into the search bar, and Google determines whether the query contains keywords that advertisers are currently bidding on. I've met business owners who like to point at extraordinarily high cost-per-click keyword categories I mentioned above such as Law, Attorneys and Insurance as a definitive example of how expensive PPC can be. However, the reality is that these keyword categories only make up a small portion of total search volumes. When planning a search engine PPC campaign, we look at long-tail keywords – as these account for the majority of web searches and can be successful with a far lower advertising budget.

In the next step, Capture, I will discuss lead pages and lead forms, but for now I will suggest that a successful advertising campaign requires careful planning to ensure your advertising budget is not wasted.

Unfortunately, I've seen too many examples of lousy landing pages that act as a single point of failure in a marketing pipeline.

PR OPPORTUNITIES

Obtaining high-profile press coverage for your business can be a great way to build authority and credibility. It's worth saying that it is rare for media coverage to result in huge sales or inbound enquiries. Many clients I've worked with that have been featured in the *Independent*, *Architecture Digest*, *Marie Claire* or *The Telegraph* see a short spike in website traffic, but unfortunately it doesn't often result in instant stardom and propel their business to the top of their industry. What I think traditional media coverage can offer is leverage. Once you've been featured in the mainstream media, you can use that in your marketing to help build credibility for your brand.

To be featured in the media, subscribe to a media enquiry service like Response Source or Help A Reporter Out (HARO). These services are a great way to connect with journalists looking for people to feature in their newspaper or magazines. You can also follow hashtags on Twitter such as #journorequest and #prrequest.

#Journorequest is a hashtag that journalists use to post requests for help with a specific story. It's also used by bloggers and podcasters, and being featured on blogs and podcasts can be a great stepping stone to getting greater media coverage – so don't underestimate the value of smaller distribution channels.

Once you see a request you think you can help with, tweet or email the journalist with the information they've asked for. The industry moves fast, so supply a sentence or two to begin with. The journalist will come back to you with further requirements if they're interested.

If you're serious about using press coverage as part of your marketing strategy, you need to think long-term. This means checking these PR platforms daily, over a series of months or even years. It's not a quick win, but it can add real value to your brand positioning.

An additional note to consider: journalists aren't in the business of writing articles or making programmes that promote small businesses (if you want that kind of coverage, you have to pay for it). What they want is to feature experts who can give their views on a topic. So rather than trying to use this to promote your business, consider how your insights and expertise can offer value. Once you've been featured in a major publication, you can integrate that coverage into your own marketing to instil trust and credibility.

ACTION LIST: CAPTIVATE

1. What is memorable about your brand? This could be a tagline or phrase, a visual part of your brand or something controversial that attracts attention
2. Create a list of keywords your customers search for online
3. What three things would solve your customer's core problems?
4. Create a database of journalists or media contacts

CHAPTER 11

Capture

Capture is the fourth C in our methodology. This is an interesting step in my tried-and-tested methodology. It's also the one that most businesses wrongly assume is the end of their marketing funnel. Many of the failed digital marketing campaigns that I've audited show that once a customer's details are captured, the marketing pipeline has ended and they've simply fed that data to their sales team to follow up with.

It's essential to understand that an effective marketing strategy goes beyond this step.

Capturing details is, of course, an essential moment in any campaign. It demonstrates that you've provided enough value to your audience and established enough trust that they feel comfortable enough to give you their name, number and email address.

This may seem basic. However, it's a significant transition from observing what you do to enquiring or taking action. Receiving contact information is a positive message to receive. To be able to capture the contact information of a prospect, you must have a landing page or lead capture form.

LEAD PAGES

A landing page is a web page for your prospects to visit to get information about a particular resource that's relevant to them. A landing page is different than your website (although it can be set up as an extension of your site). It has a single purpose – it's created explicitly for the offer you're presenting. It's used as a lead generation tool that encourages people to provide their contact information in exchange for the offer you're promoting, such as downloading your lead magnet, registering for your webinar, subscribing to your podcast or taking a quiz.

Successful landing pages will increase your conversion rates. They have the potential to make sales by growing your subscriber numbers and helping to convert visitors into leads. Building a landing page can be simple – but don't underestimate the importance of what you see on a landing page. The content should be an extension of the material your prospects have already seen. It should be perfectly crafted and optimised for opt-ins. Ideally, you will have different landing pages for each customer problem you are solving. For best results, each will focus on a particular goal: people who come to your landing page should be interested in what you have to offer and are therefore more likely to opt-in if they see consistency between the content you've been feeding them and this page. It's imperative that you meet their expectations and ensure the content they wish to access is given to them promptly. This is a great way to build trust.

A good landing page will be compelling and entice your prospect to move forward with their opt-in. You will ideally be offering something people can't resist.

The perfect landing page has these seven things:

1. Headline
2. Sub-heading
3. Lead magnet
4. Juicy copywriting
5. Social proof
6. Opt-in form
7. Call to action

Headline

Ask a burning question. Your title is the most crucial part of your landing page. This is the one part of your copy you can be 99.9% sure your prospects will read.

Sub-heading

Tease with a solution to your customer's problem. This should be simple and easy to understand – don't try to be witty or funny at this point as it may confuse your prospects.

Lead magnet

Include an image or video of what your prospect will receive. For example, focus on the value customers will get from downloading your eBook.

Juicy copywriting

The more specific and targeted your landing page is, the better. Review your copy, look for redundant passages, and edit ruthlessly to keep it bright and straightforward.

Social proof

Include awards you have won and the logos of trusted clients. Testimonials and real people's reviews of your offer will give your new prospect the confidence to take action.

Opt-in forms

Don't try to collect more information than visitors are willing to give. Most people won't give out ten different pieces of information to download your eBook. If you can get their name and email address, your landing page has successfully done its job!

Call to action

Your CTA should be significant, contrasting, and compelling. Place it above the fold of the web page, so visitors don't have to go searching for it. Make it easy for them to take action.

Your landing page must be mobile optimised. This is a mistake that I still see far too often. More than half of today's internet users will visit your landing page from a smartphone or tablet, and this number is growing. Ensure the whole page is optimised for mobile, and that includes your opt-in forms.

Although many landing pages are simple in design, it's essential to ensure your message is consistent. Just because a prospect clicks through to your page doesn't guarantee they will hand over their contact information. I was speaking to a business owner at a networking event recently, and he was boasting about how easy and cheap it was to outsource his landing page to a virtual assistant abroad. When I took a look at it, I quickly noticed how different it looked from the business card that he had given me. I also saw that there was a spelling mistake in the copy. I'm all for outsourcing jobs and tasks that don't need to be performed by the business owner, however small inconsistencies like these can be detrimental to your conversion rates. I urge you to take care of this process. If you invest the time and resources necessary for developing this on a high level, you will reap the rewards in the months ahead.

Landing page creation is an essential skill for improving conversions and moving your prospects into your nurturing campaign which we address in the fifth C, Converse.

ACTION LIST: CAPTURE

1. Decide on one giveaway
2. Create a lead page
3. Create a lead form

CHAPTER 12

Converse

Converse is the fifth C in my methodology. This step is about having conversations and strengthening the relationships you have with your prospects. It's about nurturing them and allowing them to get to know you. I often refer back to the first step, Connect, in this section because the planning has been done and now you can focus on the implementation.

Leads that have been nurtured through targeted content result in increasing final sales of upwards of 20%.

THREE WAYS TO NURTURE YOUR PROSPECTS

There are many ways to nurture prospects, but I want to focus on three core ways that are not only easy to implement but are also the quickest ways to accelerate growth in your business.

As business owners, we understand that nurturing prospects and leads is essential in business. However, how do you make sure your strategy grabs the attention of your demographic? A study by research industry experts Forrester has found that those who engaged in lead-nurturing with a strong focus saw an increase in sales by a staggering 50%.

Nurturing leads is an exercise every brand should focus on in their business. I want to show you how to break the mould and ensure your content is being consumed regularly and efficiently by your ideal audience.

Email marketing

Email marketing is not a new technique. It is, however, a technique that many businesses underutilise. Many companies send out the odd email to promote a sale, ask for feedback, or promote a product or service. I wager that not many SMEs are engaging in personalising their email marketing – probably because they are dubious on whether it works, or they lack the knowledge on how to execute it effectively while saving time and money.

The easiest way to exercise personalised email marketing is through behavioural trends. Although this can sound like a sophisticated strategy to take on, it's much more straightforward than it seems. I recommend email campaigns be implemented through automation programmes. These providers can prompt an email to be sent out at a time you choose, through the use of triggers. Triggers can include your prospect visiting specific pages on a website, spending a certain amount of time on a blog post, and many more.

The ability to combine your email marketing leads with behavioural aspects of your consumer is unrivalled in its ability to form a stronger bond between the customer and your brand. Nurturing your prospects through email marketing should be a top priority for any business looking to increase their sales.

Research by Experian has found emails that present a personalised aspect can subsequently generate upwards of six times the revenue for business over standardised emails.

I've experienced this first-hand. I was recently showing some new make-up I had purchased to my friend Sarah – I raved about how long-lasting it was and was particularly impressed by the work the brand did with animal charities. They are a vegan-friendly and cruelty-free cosmetic brand, and I encouraged my friend to test some of the make-up I had already purchased and to check them out online. Sarah began following them on Instagram and sent me a text a few weeks later to ask what shade of foundation of mine she had tried as she was now thinking about purchasing. I called her to answer her question and tell her about another product I had just tried which I thought she would like. She was gushing about their Instagram stories, and I took pride in the fact that I had introduced her to the brand. While on the phone she jumped onto their website and added the items to her shopping cart, and our conversation moved on to another topic. We were chatting away, planning the next time we would see each other before she was interrupted by her two children fighting in the background. She growled and said she needed to go, and we would catch up later.

A few days passed, and I received another text from Sarah asking for the shade of foundation because she had forgotten to place the order after the children had interrupted her. She complained that they had been a nightmare over the school holiday break and she couldn't wait for them to go back to school. On the plus side, she had received an email from the cosmetic brand reminding her about her abandoned cart and offering her a 15% off discount code. Sarah was ecstatic. Furthermore, she received two additional emails over the next week with tutorials on the different make-up looks she could create with the products she had purchased and instructions on how to win their new make-up palette by using their specific hashtag on social media.

I remember thinking this brand knows exactly what they're doing with their step five, Converse. They had successfully nurtured Sarah into a raving fan before she even received her products.

Using social media to develop relationships

You already know you should be using social media to accelerate your business, but are you using it to nurture your prospects, or are you still focused on posting for the sake of posting?

Some of the work we did in step one, Connect, will be really helpful for this part of your marketing pipeline. Using social media requires a variety of essential aspects, such as ensuring your brand remains constant throughout your content, the tone of voice is clearly defined, and the interactions reflect your brand's mission.

Technology such as social media is a crucial strategy in nurturing your marketing leads, along with your entire campaign. Social media lends itself well to original content such as blog posts, video, and audio and can help build your audience – ultimately driving more users to your website.

Interactions on your social media platforms can be tracked, evaluated, and used as research for modifying your campaigns. There are a variety of lead-scoring automation platforms that can be used to monitor your social media to ensure it remains a crucial aspect when nurturing your marketing leads.

Did you know that one active user has the potential to reach 2.7m users?

In the world of social media, we often refer to reach and generations when discussing your prospects' potential value. Depending on security settings, your prospects can give your brand an even greater reach than you ever imagined. Reach measures the spread of a social media conversation. On its own, reach can help you understand how far your content is disseminating and how big your audience is based on your current followers, connections, or likes. Reach is a measure of potential audience size, and generations refer to how you gain that reach. For example, if you have 300 connections on LinkedIn, these are considered your first-generation connections. However, you can still reach your second and third generations through engagement with your first generation. Your second generation are the people that your first generation are connected to, and your third generation is their connections.

A large audience is good, but reach alone doesn't tell you much about the success of a digital marketing campaign. Reach is used as the denominator in your social media measurement equations.

If we choose an engagement ratio, such as the number of clicks, and divide them by reach, we can calculate an engagement percentage.

If you're not a numbers person, don't worry. You can have a social media consultant or management platform generate the reports for you. I just want you to understand that social media can be measured.

I met a man named Sameer at a client's Christmas party last year. He's the owner of an insurance company, and as we got talking about what we do, he asked me about social media marketing. He said, 'I've tried a bit of social media, and my assistant keeps telling me we need to do it, but I can never think of anything to say, and when we do post something, hardly anyone likes it, and we certainly don't get any business from it.' I asked him, 'Do you write blogs that help address your client's main concerns about purchasing insurance?' 'No,' he exclaimed, 'we mostly post links to our website pages.' I asked him, 'Do you think your audience finds that interesting?' Sameer said, 'It's not interesting, but it provides basic information about our business.'

This is a problem. Sameer has assumed the people visiting his social media are already interested in purchasing from him. Not even Coca-Cola makes that assumption, and they are a multi-billion-dollar brand. Coca-Cola sponsors events, they tell stories through their video content, and they show us how fun it is to share a Coke. It's carefree and about sharing moments of optimism and happiness. Sameer is undoubtedly not the only small business owner guilty of this sort of behaviour on social media. Just because you make the effort to post a link three times a week on your social media pages doesn't mean you will generate leads via social media. You must converse with your prospects to build trust and credibility.

Sameer had his assistant join one of my webinars following our conversation; I know that she understood our six Cs methodology because she sent me a follow-up email saying how much she valued the structure. She felt confident she could help the small team at Sameer's insurance company create a pipeline that would not only attract a better customer, but also entice them to engage with the brand.

Nurturing and conversing with your audience on social media requires interesting, educational and standout content. The idea is that your audience should learn everything there is to know about what you stand for and how you go about getting results. The goal should be that they feel like you're the only business they would trust to help them solve their problem.

Reviews and testimonials

In today's world, we are surrounded by an overwhelming number of brands. Businesses, on average, are better at marketing their products and services – however it can be challenging to stand out from the crowd and rise above the noise. Reviews play an important role in purchase decisions. Your customers will look to you to understand the benefits of buying from you and to understand the range of products or services you offer. However, they will turn to online reviews for credibility. Every company says their product is the best, and while for you that may be true, consumers demand social proof. They want to hear about other people's experiences.

Acquiring reviews, recommendations and testimonials should be a top priority for all businesses. A consistent flow of reviews that explain the benefits, values, levels of customer service, and trustworthiness of your company will add credibility to your business and give your prospects the confidence to move forward in the journey through your pipeline.

I was conducting a brand audit for a client named Ian, the owner of an eclectic furniture company in Islington, North London, a few years ago. Ian was in his late forties, originally an East End lad. He did deals on a hand-shake, dealt mostly in cash sales, and delivered on his promises. His business was an edgy shop. Ian travelled and sourced objects from all over the world and sold most of his stock to wealthy homemakers and funky restaurants and hotels. Walking around the store you would find an 18th-century British prison door, neon signs from Vegas from the 1960s and sewing machines from Iraq used for mass production in the 1920s. They had a 17th-century Indian doorway, 1950s stage lights, and Murano lighting. It was a treasure trove of incredible items that interior designers obsessed over.

Ian approached me about their online brand because they were struggling to get visibility online, and their foot traffic to their store had slowed dramatically over the last few years. Alongside some of the social media work we planned to carry out, raising their profile through online reviews was top of the agenda for me. They had two prominent competitors in the area. Ian struggled to view these other companies as competitors because he didn't believe they offered products of the same quality as his. 'They're rubbish,' he said. According to Ian, 'They offer cheap rip-offs and try to confuse customers into thinking they are original pieces when customers go to their shop – but then they visit us and realise the difference.' Although this may have been true, I still called them competitors because Google believed they were. These two other furniture companies were using the same terminology online, and so for any potential customers conducting an online search, they would likely come across all three retail shops. The online reviews for these other companies were exceptional. Ian had never focused on obtaining reviews or testimonials for his company, despite having an impressive list of celebrity clientele.

He was a true offline business and said he didn't understand digital marketing or the internet. He was wary of my plan, but the sad reality was, his business was failing. He needed to make some changes.

We spent six months reaching out to previous clients for reviews and testimonials, and implemented a new automated email campaign that would prompt new and future customers to post their feedback online. Business cards and posters in-store also prompted visitors to the store to check in via social media and review the shop online. By the end of the campaign, the business had over seventy five-star reviews which significantly improved their search visibility online and made their store a must-visit business in the area. The comments about the shop were outstanding, and Ian told me they bought a tear to his eye just by reading them.

Reviews and testimonials are powerful.

EMAIL CAMPAIGNS AND TEXT MESSAGING

Email has been around for over twenty-five years, and it's not going anywhere anytime soon. Don't stress about GDPR – as long as you have acquired your prospects' data as per the GDPR guidelines you shouldn't be concerned. Email marketing is the most direct and inexpensive way to reach customers with critical information. The reason is simple – consumers are attached to their emails 24/7. Just consider for a moment how many times you've checked your email today. Most of us do this more than three times before lunchtime.

But let me be clear, not just any email will do. Successful email campaigns must be engaging, relevant, informative, and entertaining.

Each time I work with a new client I suggest our goal for this fifth C is to engage with and delight their audience. Let's consider this for a moment. We captivated their attention and offered them something juicy that encouraged them to give you their precious contact information. This is gold. It's a significant step because you now have an opportunity to build a relationship which could lead to them becoming a valuable customer.

The reason it's essential to surprise and delight them at this point is that many people are naturally sceptical. We as consumers expect that when we hand over our email address, we are going to be bombarded with lots of annoying emails.

I remember one of the first expo's I did in London for my business. We were booked to be an exhibitor at a business expo held at Kensington Olympia, and we developed an excellent package to promote at the show and were excited about the event. We also decided to run a competition at the event. It was a Wheel of Fortune, where attendees provided us with their contact info (which we scanned from their badge) in exchange for an entry to the competition. Each person would spin the wheel to immediately win a prize and go into the draw to win £1,000 worth of marketing services. As the owner of the business I thought it was a great deal – not only did everyone who participated win something immediately, but they also had the opportunity to win an even bigger prize just for providing us with their name, number, and email. It was surprising to me that the team on the stand were rejected by hundreds of attendees who said they didn't want to participate because they knew they would be bombarded with loads of emails and hated receiving them.

I felt offended by this feedback, but on reflection, I decided that we needed to ensure that the content we did push out via email was high-quality. We very rarely promote our services via our email marketing campaigns, but we offer valuable content. Materials that our prospects can use and implement in their businesses without our support. Our mantra with email is to give, give, give. If we supply great information and solutions that are easy to implement, we build trust with our prospects. Then, once their businesses have grown and they no longer have the time to create and implement their own digital marketing strategies, we are the first digital marketing agency they think about contacting, because they've been utilising our principles and recommendations.

We aim to surprise the subscribers on our email list with juicy tips and ideas of things they could implement. We delight them with a free giveaway and try to do the opposite of many of our competitors – which earns us more trust.

SOCIAL MEDIA

Conversing via social media is a non-evasive and natural way to build a relationship with your audience.

It can be very tempting to post updates about your latest promotional offer or ask for an investment. The thing about social media is that people go there to be social, not to be sold to. It's essential to keep this in mind when planning the nurturing phase of your social media strategy. There is no fixed rule on the number of posts that should be shared. Every social network is different, and your business is unique, and the truth is, you won't know what is appropriate until you start testing. I recommend starting with one post per day across your social networks. The exception to this rule is Twitter – start with a minimum of five posts or tweets per day. You will need to try posting at different times of the day, and it will be four to six weeks before you'll have enough data to see what's worked best. The critical part of nurturing your prospects via social media is the quality of the content you are posting – this is far more important than the volume of posts or the times of day. Volume and timing are secondary factors to the value you offer through content.

I was discussing social media strategy at a recent business owner's accountability group. We are a group of individuals who all run businesses in the UK, each of us works in different sectors, and we meet regularly to exchange ideas, winning business strategies, and discuss any challenges we're facing. Many of the problems the members face are marketing related. Sean is a business coach; he lacks the time needed to plan and implement a social media strategy for his business. In our meeting a few months ago, he said one of his challenges from the previous month was that his social media wasn't generating him any business. He was frustrated. When I asked him which of his customer's problems he had been trying to solve via his social media content, he had a blank look on his face. I asked if we could spend a few minutes looking at one of his social media pages as a group and see if we could determine why he wasn't getting his desired result. Sean explained he had planned out his social media posts and used a virtual assistant to create some graphics to share alongside his posts. All of this seemed like the perfect place to begin with social media. Once we looked at his social media account, we could see that the engagement levels had been low. Some of the posts didn't have any likes or comments at all.

I recently ran a workshop for an events company near Waterloo station. There were sixty attendees, and the topic for the seminar was How to Improve Engagement Levels Online. There are two core reasons that most businesses lack engagement online. The first is that the content is not attractive to their audience, and the second is that their audience doesn't use the platform they're promoting the content within.

I explained this to Sean at our accountability group meeting. I said, 'I think it is great that you are posting daily and that you took the time to plan out the posts that you wanted to share. Where I feel you could be falling short is in the quality of the posts.' People can be upset by a statement like this. To suggest that something they have produced is not of good quality often hits a nerve. This goes back to our primitive instinct to want to be accepted by our peers. We associate poor quality with products that are inexpensive and not made to last. A t-shirt for sale at Primark will be very cheap, and the quality will be poor compared to a t-shirt for sale at Ted Baker. We understand the difference in the quality of the material used and the way the item is manufactured, and therefore understand why it's valued at a higher price.

The same applies to Sean's example of his content. Content is only valuable, and therefore worthy of engagement, if it's relevant or helps to solve a problem for the customer. 'Don't be afraid to give away your best advice,' I said to Sean. 'Consider what would be helpful, relevant, and interesting to your audience. It could be a Q&A session on the biggest challenges your customers suffer from. If you shared a video clip of you answering those questions, you show off your expertise in this area, and your new prospects get to see your personality and how you coach. This type of content would be so much more powerful than the motivational quotes currently on your social media accounts.'

Once you're confident your content offers real value to your audience, you should naturally see your engagement levels increase. However, stage two to social media marketing is to actively engage with your audience and turn them into paying customers. I know a lot of small business owners posting a couple of times a day, thinking that they are doing the right thing when it comes to social media marketing. Unfortunately, you can't just post and walk away. Or perhaps more accurately, if you want to generate leads from social media, investing time into starting conversations with those that have engaged on one of your posts should be made a priority.

Flori, the investor and introducer, has done this very successfully. Her primary way to converse via social media was through video. Sharing two videos per week on LinkedIn, Facebook and IGTV established credibility with her ideal prospects. It was through video that she was able to educate her audience on the property development projects she was funding. She shared progress reports and insights into the next few developments she was reviewing. Flori claims that many of her partnerships have stemmed from investors observing her online over a period of months. Once they learn her approach to business, how she conducts herself and see her success, it becomes very simple for her to arrange a sales meeting to discuss future investment opportunities.

You must give value to build trust and nurture relationships. It's through this nurturing that you will see prime opportunities to engage with your audience, and then you can consider converting them into customers.

LEVERAGING REVIEWS

Online business reviews offer a range of benefits. They serve as incredible ranking signals for local SEO, and reviews from customers can be seen as one of the most powerful ways of promoting trust and confidence in your business. To highlight this, a recent survey from Zendesk found that 90% of respondents claimed that positive reviews affected their purchasing decisions.

Reviews matter when it comes to attracting new prospects and helping them choose between your company and your competition.

Leveraging reviews and testimonials should be an essential element of your nurturing strategy. At this point, you've given your audience rich content that offers them value, you've shown them who you are and what you stand for, and you've spent a lot of time and resources educating them. Reviews offer tremendous value because they come from a third party. It's a non-biased representation of your business. A real person who has done business with you has taken the time to provide insight into their experience. The amount of confidence this will give any prospect of yours that is sitting-on-the-fence or being indecisive is incredible.

Storytelling is an essential element to successful reviews. To obtain a review or testimonial that offers real value to your business, it must tell a story. Compare the two reviews below.

> Attending *Property Success Live* allowed me to get clarity on my property investing strategy and common pitfalls to look out for when stacking a deal. I had so many breakthrough moments and now feel clear on how to move forward. Investing in personal development and training is invaluable. I would recommend this course.

> Or,
>
> Before *Property Success Live*, I was viewing potential investment properties every weekend in my local area. I was regularly putting in offers, but nothing was being accepted, and I was offending estate agents with my low offers. It felt impossible to find below market value properties. Thanks to the practical tips and strategies I learned at the event, I am clear on the type of properties I need to view and how to present my offers to agents in a way that makes sense to them. I've built relationships with two agents who now bring property deals to me, and I have closed three deals in the last three months.

Example one says lots of nice things, but example two is much more effective because a transformational story has been told. The person in the second example has been on a journey and provided tangible results. It's much easier to relate to the person in example two because they've told us what their problem was before attending, and then what the outcome has been from investing in the event.

It can take some time to get this right, and there will be times that you need to ask your audience specific questions to get them to structure their testimonials in this way. I learned this the hard way. In the past,

I would ask clients to write a review or to record a video testimonial for me and leave them to say whatever felt comfortable for them. Everybody said lovely things, but there were often a lot of juicy details missing. A client of mine that provided me with a video testimonial told me a few months later in one of our marketing strategy meetings that it had been difficult to provide the testimonial. She said she had really thought about what to say and recorded it over and over again, and now when she sees it played back, she doesn't think she makes a significant impact. As we were going through her marketing strategy and reporting from the last quarter, she said, 'See, this is the stuff I should have been talking about in the testimonial! I just waffled on about how much I love your team – how is that helpful?'

I realised at that moment that another client had made a similar comment. I felt terrible that it had caused them so much stress. I thought creating a testimonial would only take them a few minutes and felt so much guilt when I learned that they had spent so long on something purely because I had asked, and they wanted to help me.

Since then I've established a set of questions and examples of good vs great testimonials, just as you see in the *Property Success Live* event example above. Here is how this has transformed one of my testimonials.

Example one:

> I would recommend Brandlective to any company that wants to have a foothold in their marketing. They are really personable and take the time to understand your business. I feel like they really care. Brandlective has done wonderful things with my social media and now I feel like we have a strong brand identity online. They are professional and have the marketing expertise that leads to great results. I wish I had hired them years ago.

Example two:

> Before hiring Brandlective, I had outsourced part of my marketing to a virtual assistant, and I was doing the rest of it myself. Although the design elements were great, I had a language barrier to deal with which meant I needed to step in and check a lot of the copy and social media posts. I was trying to do a lot of content myself too which was inconsistent because I was trying to juggle so many other things in my business. After meeting with Stacey and the team at Brandlective, I realised how much more I could be achieving. They clearly articulate my message, the content is rich and enticing, and my social media is actually generating tangible results. It's been six months since our campaign launched

> and our social media following has increased by 1124% and engagement on each post has increased. Our web traffic has tripled, and we receive leads daily. Brandlective's Social Media Kickstarter package is a must for businesses looking to grow.

All of this information is true; our client just didn't know how to articulate it correctly in her original testimonial. All the information in example one is really lovely, it's a good review but it doesn't show my prospects how our services can transform their digital marketing.

The ideal testimonial or review needs to show the pain point, show how your product or service has healed the pain, and what the tangible result was after working with you. It's best to show the result in statistics if possible.

What problem were you suffering from?

With local search results, search engines such as Google will often show a series of businesses in the area. It's when these searches are conducted that your potential customers will see things like your website, address, phone number, and of course reviews that consumers have written about your business. These reviews can help you with your click-through rate, but they can also help your business appear in the search results in the first place.

ACTION LIST: CONVERSE

1. Register an email marketing account with a service like Mailchimp
2. Choose two topics your audience would pay to learn more about, and focus thirty days of social media content addressing these two topics
3. Claim profiles on top review sites in your sector
4. Ask five customers for reviews

CHAPTER 13

Convert

Convert is the sixth C in my methodology. This is the time to sell. Businesses that attempt to convert prospects earlier in this pipeline will always fail at digital marketing. They alienate their audience by trying to sell before enough trust is built. This is not word of mouth. When a customer is referred to you by a current customer or a friend, there's enough social proof to convert that prospect on the spot. Word of mouth is a fantastic strategy both when you're launching a new business and when you've built an empire and you can leverage your brand power. After your first year in business, you will likely need to leverage a digital marketing strategy to generate fresh inbound leads every day. When you're generating leads online you need to nurture prospects; they need to know, like and trust you before they will convert to a paying customer.

I see too many businesses attempting to sell to prospects during step two and three. Even more people try to sell at step five – they believe it's a sign to sell once a prospect has provided their contact information. There will always be exceptions to the rule, but for the vast majority of businesses, when generating cold leads they need a warm nurturing period before they're ready to part with their hard-earned money. This is particularly true for big-ticket items.

Last year I was working with a property developer to help them locate investors. They were seeking £100k to £1m in financing. Of course, there are people out there that will take a gamble and invest vast amounts of money on a whim, but they are few and far between. An individual who doesn't know you or your brand will want to do their due diligence before investing in a project. Following this six Cs methodology, we were able to clearly articulate what the business stood for and built a trustworthy and professional brand. The content we created allowed potential investors to download investor kits from the brand's website, and video interviews with the developer at every phase of the project showed prospects their approach and how the developer carried himself. The developer's knowledge and confidence shone through. Q & A blog posts were shared across a Facebook and LinkedIn advertising campaign. Prospects who read these blog posts were prompted with a lead form to download case studies and register for networking events. Weekly newsletters and project updates were shared via email and the brand's social media accounts were filled with fascinating insights from the project, the local area, industry news, media coverage, and more video content. The prospects were given ample time to get to know the developer and the project, trust was established, and landing investment became a much smoother process for the developer. Even prospects who didn't invest in this project are more aware of the brand and may be converted on the next one. They will also have this brand front of mind to refer friends or associates who are interested in investment opportunities.

This six-step process is just that: a process. It's not a quick way to win business, it's a strategy. It's created to build a pipeline of inbound enquiries while raising the profile of your brand. You must be patient, you must know that there is a demand for what you're offering, you must be clear on who your audience is, and you must provide them with value. When implemented correctly, it's a game changer.

One other point I would like to make is that it's important to have a salesperson or business development manager whose job it is to convert the sale. Once you have a flow of inbound leads and enquiries, it's essential to be ready to sell. Over the last ten years,

I've observed two types of business owners: the over-eager sales person that doesn't want to waste their time with a marketing funnel and wants to jump right in and sell, and the ones on the opposite end of the spectrum who want marketing to make the sale for them.

Sales and marketing are closely interlinked, which is why it's sometimes so confusing as to which should do what. They are both aimed at increasing revenue for a business. In small companies, it can often become a blurred line because team members usually wear more than one hat in the business. Large companies and corporations make clear distinctions between sales and marketing, and it's common to have specialised people handling them independently. I think it's important to look at sales and marketing in the same way a large business does. Even if your small business has the same person handling both responsibilities, it's important to be able to separate them to understand how to obtain the best outcome.

In general, marketing has a long lead time, while sales pertain to shorter goals. As we have discussed in our six Cs model, marketing involves a longer process of building and establishing a brand. In marketing, we aim to raise awareness of the brand and entice prospects to engage. This is different from the sales function which is a short process of converting the prospect into a customer.

Marketing can be used as a footboard for sales. It warms up your prospects and prepares the salesperson to approach individuals to convert into a customer or client.

TRACKING RESULTS

Monitoring how your digital marketing efforts are performing is essential. Knowing exactly how prospects are finding your content and which content they are interacting with will help you to evolve your strategy. The constant evolution of a digital marketing strategy will ensure your ROI improves across every facet of your campaign.

Google Analytics is a powerful tool to use to monitor and report on your campaign performance. Through the use of Google Analytics, you will see a vast amount of data about your website that can be used to enhance the performance of your marketing funnel.

I was working with a client in London who was running a content marketing campaign across social media platforms. When I was first brought on to consult and create a pay-per-click campaign for her, she said she had no idea where the sales were coming from, but she suspected it was Facebook. That is where she received the most engagement. She said: 'I love my Instagram page, it looks beautiful, and I get a lot of likes, but I don't think people actually buy anything they see on Instagram.' When I asked her if she was using Google Analytics to monitor her inbound traffic, she said no. She said, 'I'm not interested in where the sales come from as long as they keep coming.' I'm by no means a numbers person, but not reporting on where a brand's website traffic is coming from, particularly when it comes to e-commerce, is crazy. As it turned out, almost 34.1% of sales were direct clicks from Instagram, 18.9% from Facebook, 6% from Pinterest and the rest from a range of organic sources.

Google Analytics can answer the following questions for you:

- How many people visit my website?
- How did my visitors find my website?
- Where do my visitors live?
- What marketing tactics have driven the most traffic to my site?
- Which pages on my website are the most popular?
- What did my visitors look at on my website?
- How can I improve my website's speed?
- What blog content do my visitors like the most?

For those unfamiliar with Google Analytics, when you log in for the first time it can be overwhelming.

With so much data available to review, it can be challenging to know where to start and how to find the most important metrics for your business.

The back end of Google Analytics is broken down into eight main sections: Dashboards, Shortcuts, Intelligence Events, Real Time, Audience, Acquisition, Behaviour and Conversions.

Many of my clients often say they find Google Analytics very confusing and difficult to navigate. Without knowing which sections to review, it's easy to waste a lot of time just trying to understand the insights.

However, when leveraged correctly, Google Analytics can provide invaluable insight into who has visited your website, how they got there in the first place, and which of your site pages they spent the most time on. These insights are powerful metrics for you to understand which parts of your strategy are working well, and which parts need to be reviewed and enhanced.

A step further for those looking for a deeper understanding is to integrate Google Webmaster Tools.

Webmaster Tools provides insights Google Analytics can't offer, such as information about the links pointing to your site, impression data, index issues, and even organic search keyword impression and click data. If you connect your Webmaster Tools account with your Analytics account, you'll gain access to new reports such as Queries, Landing Pages and Geographical Summary.

MARKETING AUTOMATION

Marketing automation refers to software that helps automate marketing functions. Many marketing agencies, including my own, will opt to automate repetitive tasks such as emails, social media, and other website actions. This allows us to spend more time creating quality content and looking at the performance of a campaign, rather than getting bogged down in the administrative tasks associated with sending emails manually or posting natively on a social media account.

Recently I've been asked if I'm concerned that marketing automation might one day make me redundant. Unlike automating manufacturing jobs or processes, utilising a marketing automation system won't make having a real-life marketer irrelevant. It does however make us more effective and productive if set up in the right way. It frees up my time, while not compromising the authenticity of the content I create. It's worth considering integrating some automation to scale your business or if you need to buy back some of your time.

For most of my clients the ultimate goal with marketing is to generate more revenue for their businesses.

Where marketing automation makes a big impact is the conversion and closure stages of this process. It can monitor the buying process and alter the journey your customers take depending on how they interact with your content. By delivering highly-targeted, personalised messages that address your prospects' specific barriers to purchase, I can improve my conversion rates.

If this is difficult to follow, consider this example with regards to email marketing.

Step one: I send an email invitation to my contacts to download one of my new lead magnets (I always send these to a targeted list of contacts that have been segmented by a previous action they have taken).

Step two: I send a follow-up thank you note to all the people that downloaded my offer.

Step three: A few days later, I send a follow-up email to the list of people who downloaded the lead magnet, pointing them to a case study relating to the same topic.

Step four: Finally, when someone visits that case study, my sales team receives a notification so they can follow up with that specific contact.

This type of automation is a great way to ensure that you don't bombard your contact list with emails they're not interested in. A prospect who has gone through this pipeline is much more qualified, and this means your sales team can focus on contacting warm leads.

A similar example of marketing automation is chatbots. Short for chat robot, this is a computer program that simulates human conversation, or chat, through artificial intelligence. Typically, a chatbot will communicate with a real person and provide them with the information they seek.

AI-based bots use natural language processes of either text or voice to figure out what the user wants. The classic example is asking Alexa to play the latest news or tell you about today's weather.

Chatbots are increasing in popularity due to the sense of immediacy that they offer. As a busy business owner, I will opt-in to anything that makes my job a little easier. I can use chatbots to share timely reminders and links to my prospects when and where they need it. For example, if someone registers for one of my webinars, they will receive a message saying, 'Click this button, and my chatbot, Julie, will remind you on Facebook Messenger when the webinar is starting.' When it's time for the webinar, my chatbot reminder makes the recipient's phone vibrate and provides a link directly to my webinar. Why is this so important? Well for starters, it increases the ROI on my webinar. Automation is important for a growing business because it means that there is less manual administrative work to do.

Marketing automation is about the ability to target contacts and send them content that is based on their behaviour. We are giving our audience the information they need, when they want it. Through this automation, I'm easing their buying decision. And as a result, my conversion rates (and revenue) benefit.

Finally, the importance of implementing an automation platform that results in identifying and targeting each customer avatar, which can be measured and adapted as time passes, is invaluable.

ACTION LIST: CONVERT

- Set up Google Analytics on your website
- Write a list of the repetitive tasks you do and consider if any of them could be automated
- Is there a list of FAQs that a chatbot could help answer for your customers?

PART THREE

CHAPTER 14

What's Next

THE EVOLUTION OF YOUR DIGITAL MARKETING STRATEGY

Don't expect to be able to use the same marketing strategy forever. How often you should evaluate your marketing and make amendments to your marketing depends on your business. It's important to thoroughly test an approach in order to decide which parts are working and which are not. This is an important factor, as I witness many small businesses who stop running Google AdWords after a week because it hasn't generated their (often unrealistic) expectations. Evolving is key. If something doesn't work the first time, chances are it will need to be updated and tested again (rather than stopping altogether). Of course, every twelve months you should be looking at your overall strategy and evaluating how it will change in the next year.

Has your business and the niche you operate in evolved in the last twelve months? Have you reviewed how you're allocating your marketing budget? Is one part of your business showing more growth potential than another? Does your marketing budget allow for innovation and the option to try something new? Are your tried-and-true tactics still working?

Your annual review of your marketing strategy should be seen through the lens of what we need versus what-we've-always done. If you're not achieving the desired result, it's not always about spending more money. Your marketing budget may be sufficient to meet your objectives; it may just need to be reallocated.

Inevitably, your business circumstances change, sometimes dramatically, and it's very common for marketing plans to change. The six Cs methodology we've been reviewing is a fantastic blueprint for your marketing strategy. You will have noticed a few things along the way. In step one, we identified how you would connect with your audience. Your audience! Not my audience, or your friend's business' audience. Your audience. It's unique and specific to your business model. There may be opportunities out there for you to mimic another business' audience, but even so, your product, service or offering will be different, therefore your marketing strategy will be unique to you. While following this blueprint, you will need to inject your business objectives into it and do the research into the requirements of your audience to get a great result.

In step two, you will create content for your audience. In your first marketing plan, you may choose to focus on video clips and blog posts. Later you may evolve your strategy to include a podcast and some content-heavy lead magnets. The evolution of step three, Captivate, may begin with Facebook adverts but require shifting towards LinkedIn as you understand your audience in more detail. How you choose to capture details in step four may change too. It's important to use the blueprint to guide your strategy, but as I've mentioned before, your marketing strategy will be unique. The platforms many of my clients use to converse with their prospects for step five change constantly. GDPR has shifted many businesses strategies away from email and towards social media. I guarantee in another few months, market conditions will shift, and you may need to follow your prospects to a new platform to ensure you can achieve the objective of step six and convert them into paying customers.

Your marketing strategy will need to evolve and adapt. Don't be afraid of this – embrace it. If you can respond to market conditions quickly, your business will thrive online.

There are so many tactics available to us as business owners today that it's easy to lose sight of the most important thing – your marketing objectives. Are the tactics you're choosing aligned with the goals you've set for your business? And are those goals still appropriate in the market today? Reviewing these questions regularly will ensure you keep your marketing strategy up to date and evolve it as required.

WHY CRITICISM IS GOOD

Criticism in the form of reviews, posts, and direct messages will happen at some point. You will never appeal to 100% of people. I encourage you to be bold, to have opinions, to stand up for what you're passionate about and take any feedback or criticism as an indicator that you're improving your visibility and creating a niche for yourself.

Criticism may not always be easy to hear (or read). However, it can be a positive thing. It allows you to examine if what you've said or posted online is in line with what you believe and feel strongly is true. If not, then there is a great lesson to be learned. If it is, then that's great – this could be the start of an interesting debate that leads to more exposure for you, both across your own social media platforms and perhaps even in traditional media.

I enjoyed a heated discussion on Twitter which stemmed from an article in *The Sun* about Kirstie Allsopp's view on travelling with children. She had commented that she and her partner Ben will occasionally travel in Premium Economy when flying abroad and keep her children in Economy. She was quoted as saying she didn't want them to be spoiled and that they should understand what it's like to work hard before enjoying the privilege of luxury travel. It sparked a frenzy online. Some were in full support of Kirstie's parenting style and claimed they do the same while travelling. While on the other side of the argument were those that were outraged that she would leave her children in Economy unsupervised (they were fifteen and eighteen years old at the time). One woman said if she had the money, she would put her children in Premium or Business and she would sit in Economy with her husband because she thinks it's important to put your children's comfort before your own. That escalated the debate; many people said that if they have paid the extra money to travel Premium or Business that they don't want to be disturbed by children. As it turned out, Kirstie Allsopp had been slightly misquoted, and she shared her original email to the journalist who had asked her for a comment. The statement showed why they chose to do that on a recent trip and how much her teenage sons loved the independence on that flight.

Having a bold opinion on a subject can generate criticism, but it can also raise your profile and lead to future opportunities. I speak to entrepreneurs and business owners all the time who don't want to risk receiving criticism online. I appreciate that there are sensitive subjects that should be avoided. However, when it comes to business if you have a clear purpose and vision and if you are confident your method, service, or product solves a problem for your audience then you must make your voice heard. Don't worry about the criticism; it may never happen. And if it does, then you can learn to leverage it to give you the limelight to grow your business.

IT'S NOT TOO LATE TO START A DIGITAL MARKETING CAMPAIGN

You haven't missed the boat. It's not too late to embrace digital marketing. I meet small business owners every day who struggle to decide which kind of marketing to do. Maybe their budgets only stretch so far, or they've always done direct mail and fear leaving it behind. Some still don't know which type of marketing will give them the most bang for their buck and their desired results. How will they measure the performance of their marketing? Who should they trust to manage their marketing? Should they do it themselves? Or should they outsource?

As a business owner, you will always have questions and hundreds of reasons why you don't want to try something new. Fear is common, and it's normal. We are fearful of trying new things for our businesses because we don't know what the outcome will be. I have new clients tell me all the time how out of control they feel because of their lack of digital marketing knowledge. I always respond with: 'The game is constantly changing. This is a great thing because it means it's never too late to learn and embrace digital marketing and social media.'

You might even be able to argue that you're in a stronger place because you're learning what is current. You're using digital platforms that are working today. I've met so many people that have worked in SEO for more than fifteen years and still use old tactics that don't actually work anymore. I was speaking at an event in London on personal brand development, and a core part of my presentation was three tips on how to manage trolls online and work with review sites to have inappropriate content removed. After my presentation, a delegate approached me in the break room and said that two of my tips were not true. He said he had worked in online sentiment and reputation management for thirteen years and that it wasn't possible to have posts removed from online platforms. He was so serious and hysterically quoted the terms and conditions of some of the largest social media platforms on the web. I turned to my colleague who was at the event to support me and I asked her, 'How many reviews did you successfully remove for clients last month?' She said, 'I had seven comments removed, but as a team, we successfully negotiated the removal of thirty-seven comments and reviews throughout the month of March.'

I turned back to the gentleman and said, he was right, it's not always possible to remove unsavoury content and there are many reasons a website will decline your request. I'm acutely aware that I've only been doing this for eight years but the information I provided was accurate, and I know that it's true, because we do it every day in my digital marketing agency.

Reputation management is a controversial service. Many people have firm opinions on this subject. How online reviews should be handled, freedom of speech, the right to be forgotten – it's a hot topic.

The event delegate continued to challenge me on the suggestions I had made during my presentations and made my team members very uncomfortable. He was confident that his level of experience outweighed my knowledge on the subject. I didn't have the decades of experience that he had in this sector. However, I'm someone who challenges the status quo. Just because something has always been done one way doesn't mean it's the only way to do it.

I'm a competitive person which is likely the reason I'm so successful with digital marketing and reputation management. The sales agency I worked in following my redundancies worked with a PR firm to handle media stories and reviews online. The PR firm was working on one review for us that had been published on a nasty blog about sales agents that worked on commission. They had concluded that nothing could be done about it. The PR team suggested that we work on optimising our own digital content to offer a balanced view to our audience.

I agree with maintaining a transparent and balanced insight into a business's culture. In fact, I now regularly work with clients to help them produce content to help solve some of their prospects' most significant challenges and highlight the benefits of working with their company. However, I didn't believe that it was impossible to remove such a damaging and untrue statement from this blog. My competitive side took over, and I took it on as my secret project. I read all about local defamatory laws and drilled down into the blog's terms of service until I found a loophole. I spent months negotiating with the site, and in the end, I managed to have the content removed. They may have declined the first thirty-six arguments I made to have it removed, but it was my thirty-seventh attempt that was successful. I didn't study law. I don't pretend to be an expert in the radically changing digital economy. But I do believe that you can learn anything you want to. I embraced the challenge of learning reputation management to help support my employer.

Some people look down on me for being self-taught. There are individuals who value their education and the length of time that they've worked in a specific industry over the actual value they deliver. Just like the event delegate who thought he knew best because he'd been doing this longer than I had been. I'm sure there are many things he knows that I don't. However, I feel confident that what I teach is what I know.

Now is the time to educate yourself, try new things online and get familiar with digital marketing. It will be a phenomenal way to reach new prospects. You can reach a local demographic while simultaneously gaining an international awareness. The ability to tailor your strategy by a campaign to get in front of a specific demographic, such as gender, location, age and interests, has never been easier. By following this six Cs method, you will be able to feed content to your audience in whichever format they enjoy.

Digital marketing is the future, and it has already become more cost effective than traditional marketing. The data recorded through tools such as Google Analytics and most social media platforms mean a campaign's success can be tracked and measured in real time – allowing you to adapt in-market campaigns for the best results. Old-school traditional marketing methods can't compete on this level. As business owners, we no longer need to wait for weeks to receive calls from a leaflet drop we did. At a touch of a button, a report can show us who has visited our websites at what time and what they were reading on the site.

I'm particularly passionate about digital marketing because I firmly believe it levels the playing field. Any business of any size can compete with even the world's biggest brands when they have a robust strategy in place. Creating content is cheap and straightforward. By creating an exceptional customer journey, you can build a strong online relationship with existing and future customers. Not to mention the brand development and awareness opportunities digital marketing provides.

I will often ask my clients considering switching from traditional methods to digital how often their sales flyers get passed around instantly by their prospects. They have no statistics. Digital marketing means you can use social share buttons and within a few seconds a prospect can share a post, promotion, or deal with all of their friends and family. The average Facebook user has 190 friends. Levels of exposure change with each of Facebook's algorithm updates, but on average 12% of those 190 friends see that person's liked posts – fifteen new prospects have seen your one message. That's before considering whether they've commented on the post (which will increase the reach of the original post even further) or if any of those fifteen prospects have also chosen to share your post, which would make that audience even more prominent. The possibilities online are endless.

Acknowledgements

This book wouldn't have been possible without the help and support of many extraordinary people.

Firstly, thank you to my Mum, Debbie, for your positivity. You've shown me such an incredible work ethic, inspiration and have never put limits on what I can achieve.

Thank you to my partner, Ross, for putting up with my obsession with work and being the most supportive, loving and encouraging human I know.

Thanks also to my sister, Rebecca, and brother Sean, for your craziness, silliness and weirdness and for always giving me a reality check into what is important; to my Brandlective superteam, you are awesome! Thank you for embracing my ideas, building my vision from behind the scenes and zigzagging with me all the way to the top.

Thank you to my mentors: Josh Cote, Sara Beth Cote, Daniel Priestley and my accountability partners – each of you has helped me in ways you can't imagine. Thank you for showing me new ways to do business, pushing me to think bigger and encouraging me through the tough bits.

And thank you to my publishers: Lucy, Joe, Anke and Kate. I've demanded so much of your time, but your advice has helped me so much. Thank you for taking on this project.

Big thanks to my broader family and friends: grandparents, aunties, uncles, cousins and childhood friends; you've helped to foster and shape my entrepreneurial spirit and inspire me in so many ways.

The digital marketing method in this book has come from many wonderful projects with amazing friends, business owners and entrepreneurs. Thank you all for allowing me the opportunity to cultivate adventure in your marketing, test my theories and take bold risks. You've kept my spark burning for digital marketing and I can't wait for the next part of the journey to unfold.

And finally, thank you, to you – the reader. For picking up and reading this book and putting your business on a path which I know will result in phenomenal things.

The Author

Stacey Kehoe has worked in digital marketing and brand development for the last ten years. She's a podcast host and editor of the SME marketing magazine *The Vault,* which has gained her media recognition and award nominations. Since establishing her first business, digital agency Brandlective Communications Ltd, in 2012, Stacey has built over 500 websites, brands, and marketing campaigns.

Regularly hired as a consultant, social media trainer, and speaker, Stacey developed the Six-Step Digital Marketing Methodology after being approached by client after client let down by other agencies who failed to implement a strategy that generated the desired results. This methodology is used at Brandlective to facilitate campaign development and enhance the speed at which their clients gain measurable results.

Stacey's vision is that those with an entrepreneurial spirit should have the resources to rise above the noise, stand out from the crowd, and show their audience who they really are. These beliefs tie in with her commitment to equality.

Stacey is leading a movement called #1MillionDays: An initiative to reduce inequality through social, economic, and political inclusion of all people.

Connect with Stacey Kehoe
LinkedIn: Stacey Kehoe
www.staceykehoe.com
www.1milliondays.com

Connect with Brandlective
Facebook: Brandlective
www.brandlective.com

Printed in Great Britain
by Amazon

41151158R00122